Contents

W9-BUU-038

Fundamentals of Academic Writing

Linda Butler

Holyoke Community College

PEARSON
Longman

Fundamentals of Academic Writing

Pearson Education, 10 Bank Street, White Plains, NY 10606

Staff credits: The people who made up the *Fundamentals of Academic Writing* team, representing editorial, production, design, and manufacturing, are: Rhea Banker, John Beaumont, Wendy Campbell, Elizabeth Carlson, Gina DiLillo, Christine Edmonds, Laura Le Dréan, Linda Moser, Edith Pullman, Kim Steiner, and Paula Van Ells.

Cover design: Jill Lehan

Cover images: (left) Mike Caldwell/Getty Images. (right) Computer circuit board, close-up (digital composite) by Jan Franz. Collection: Stone. Getty Images.

Text composition: Integra

Text font: 13/14.5 Times Roman

Illustrator credits: Steve Attoe (16, 17, 63, 68, 70, 156, 165, 192); Suzanne Mogensen (2, 3, 5, 23, 60, 104, 106, 107, 145, 185); Jill Wood (9, 45, 51, 55, 57, 58, 64, 74, 80, 92, 95, 100, 112, 126, 167, 195);

Photo credits: p. 1 Art Vandalay/Getty Images; p. 6 Jason Horowitz/zefa/Corbis; p. 18 Jack Fields/Corbis; p. 22 (top) Paul Hardy/Corbis; p. 22 (bottom) Craig Tuttle/Corbis; p. 27 Steve Smith/Getty Images; p. 42 Michael Prince/Corbis; p. 52 Images.com/Corbis; p. 53 Michael Prince/Corbis; p. 56 (top) Design Pics/Royalty-Free/Fotosearch; p. 56 (middle) JupiterImages/Comstock; p. 56 (bottom) Bill Varie/Corbis; p. 57 Tim Boyle/2005 Getty Images; p. 71 (top left) JupiterImages/Comstock; p. 71 (top right) JupiterImages/Comstock; p. 71 (bottom left) Brand X Pictures/JupiterImages/Comstock; p. 71 (bottom right) JupiterImages/Comstock; p. 76 Simon Marcus/Corbis; p. 84 Royalty-Free/Corbis; p. 86 Myron Jay Dorf/Corbis; p. 89 Creatas/JupiterImages/Comstock; p. 97 Royalty-Free/Corbis; p. 98 (left) George Shelley/Corbis; p. 98 (right) Royalty-Free/Corbis; p. 102 Royalty-Free/Corbis; p. 109 (top left) Tim Garcha/zefa/Corbis; p. 109 (top right) Digital Vision/Royalty-Free/Fotosearch; p. 109 (bottom left) Royalty-Free/Corbis; p. 109 (bottom right) Ed Bock/Corbis; p. 114 (top left) Joaquin Palting/Corbis; p. 114 (top right) Royalty-Free/Corbis; p. 114 (bottom left) Gareth Brown/Corbis; p. 114 (bottom right) Simon Marcus/Corbis; p. 117 Vincent/zefa/Corbis; p. 119 Wally McNamee/Corbis; p. 122 (top) Dave G. Houser/Post-Houserstock/Corbis; p. 122 (bottom) Tim Davis/Corbis; p. 137 Tom Stewart/Corbis; p. 144 Fridmar Damm/zefa/Corbis; p. 147 Patrik Giardino/Corbis; p. 154 Bettmann/Corbis; p. 161 B. Bird/zefa/Corbis; p. 166 Dave G. Houser/Post-Houserstock/Corbis; p. 169 Royalty-Free/Corbis; p. 172 Patrik Giardino/Corbis; p. 180 Royalty-Free/Corbis; p. 189 David Pu'u/Corbis; p. 193 Jules Perrier/Corbis; p. 196 Barry Lewis/Corbis

Library of Congress Cataloging-in-Publication Data

Butler, Linda.
  Fundamentals of academic writing / Linda Butler.
    p.   cm.
  Includes index.
  ISBN 0-13-199557-X (student book : alk. paper) — ISBN 0-13-613390-8 (answer key : alk. paper)
  1. English language—Textbooks for foreign speakers.   2. English language—Rhetoric—Problems, exercises, etc.   3. Academic writing—Problems, exercises, etc.   4. English language—Grammar—Problems, exercises, etc.
  I. Title.
PE1128.B854 2006
428.6'4—dc22
                                                                                        2006032582

Printed in the United States of America
4 5 6 7 8 9 10—BAH—10 09 08

APPENDICES

Preface

Fundamentals of Academic Writing is intended for beginning-level students learning English as a second or foreign language in college, adult, or secondary school programs. It offers a carefully structured approach that helps students develop basic writing skills, understand writing as a process, and build a solid foundation for becoming confident, independent writers in English.

To the Instructor

The text offers a wealth of realistic models to inspire and guide student writers. It also features clear explanations of sentence structure, grammar, and mechanics, followed by the extensive practice students need to assimilate the material and write with accuracy. The text focuses on the elements of good sentences but within the context of simple descriptive and narrative paragraphs on student-centered topics. It effectively combines an introduction to basic paragraph structure with an emphasis on personal writing, the kind of writing that is most appropriate and motivating for learners at the beginning level. There are interactive tasks throughout the text—pair work, small-group activities, and full-class discussions—that engage students in the learning process and complement the solitary work that writers must do. There are also directions for keeping a journal, with plentiful suggestions for journal-entry topics, so that students write for fluency building in addition to doing the more formal assignments. Finally, the extensive appendices and thorough index make the text a valuable and easy-to-use reference tool.

Organization of the Text

Fundamentals of Academic Writing takes students from a look at the big picture to practice of specific elements and then to creating their own paragraphs, where they put together everything they have learned. The text has an introduction (Getting Started) followed by nine chapters and the appendices. Each Chapter Opener page includes a photograph and the chapter title to introduce the theme, and it also outlines the chapter's contents. The chapters are organized as follows:

Chapter Preview

Each chapter begins with a Chapter Preview that includes two simple model paragraphs which let students see exactly where they are headed. The models use structures and vocabulary that are easy for beginners to understand and emulate. The questions following the models draw the students' attention first to content and organization and then to certain features of the writers' language, such as verb forms, transition signals, key vocabulary, and so on.

Organization	The second section of each chapter is devoted to organization. In the early chapters, students learn what sentences and paragraphs are and how their papers should look. Later chapters deal with the elements of standard paragraph structure, patterns of organization within paragraphs (such as chronological order), and writers' strategies for organizing their ideas.
Sentence Structure/ Grammar/ Mechanics/ Vocabulary	Four strands—Sentence Structure, Grammar, Mechanics, and Vocabulary—combine in various ways, always with a focus on writing at the word and sentence level. You will find brief, clear explanations followed by valuable practice in the nuts and bolts of effective and accurate writing.

- *Sentence Structure*. Students first learn to identify subjects and verbs. Then they progress through four patterns of simple sentences, followed by compound sentences with *and*, *but*, and *so*, and finally, a brief introduction to complex sentences with time clauses.
- *Grammar*. Students focus initially on the basic parts of speech and later on the structures that will be most useful to them in writing the assigned paragraph for that chapter. For example, they study the verb tenses needed to write about everyday life (simple present), describe ongoing activities (present progressive), relate past events (simple past), and write about the future (*be going to* and *will*).
- *Mechanics*. Students learn such basics as elementary rules for capitalization, end punctuation, titles, and commas.
- *Vocabulary*. Students further their understanding of the parts of speech and broaden their vocabulary base, particularly in ways that will help them with the assigned writing.

The Writing Process	In Chapter 1, students learn the term *process*, and they get an overview of the writing process. In Chapter 2, they learn the specific steps they will take as they plan, compose, and finalize their paragraphs. In Chapters 2 through 9, students are guided step by step through the process of writing the assigned paragraph, initially with substantial support, later with increasing demands on their own creativity. By consistently following these steps, they learn how to tackle a writing assignment.
Expansion Activities	This concluding section of each chapter has two goals: (1) to encourage journal writing and (2) to provide additional paragraph-writing tasks. The latter can provide further practice for the entire class or serve as extra assignments for those students ready to work independently.

Teaching Suggestions

The Getting Started section offers a good icebreaker at the start of a course. It helps students get to know one another by interviewing, introducing, and writing about a classmate. In addition, its three sections—Prewriting, Writing, and Sharing—anticipate the writing process students will follow. If you collect the students' papers, I suggest you do not correct them but rather keep the focus on content at this point. Consider holding on to the papers until the end of the course, when seeing them again can serve as a delightful reminder to students of how far they have come.

Begin each chapter with a close look at the model paragraphs. Two models are provided in each case so that students can see more than one way of addressing a writing task and have ample material to guide them as they create their paragraphs. The questions about the models are intended for work in pairs or small groups, to be followed by teacher-led full-class discussion. You may wish to do further analysis of the models—comparing and contrasting the writers' choices, vocabulary, and so on—as appropriate for your class.

As you continue in the chapter, remember that with beginning-level students, it is particularly helpful for you to read explanations and directions aloud or have capable student readers do so. Throughout the text, you will notice direction lines that say, "Work alone or with a partner." You can leave it up to the individual student whether to collaborate with a classmate or go it alone, or you can assign students to do the exercises as you think best. Sometimes the directions tell students to take a piece of paper because the exercise requires them to write their own sentences, which you will probably want to collect.

An introduction to journal writing appears on page 25, at the end of Chapter 1, but you can take your students to this section even sooner or wait until later in the course if you prefer. Journals are a wonderful way to get students writing about what interests them and give them a safe place to experiment with English as they search for new ways to express themselves. I recommend responding solely to the content of journal entries, ignoring errors (but writing questions if the content is unclear) in order to lessen the writer's performance anxiety and emphasize writing to communicate. With the writer's permission, I read aloud to the class the occasional journal entry that is especially thoughtful, funny, or intriguing, a practice that rewards the writer and can inspire others. Journal entries can also provide topics for more formal paragraph assignments. Teachers sometimes find journals time-consuming, but remember that you need not collect journals after every entry, collect all journals on the same day, or respond to entries at length. (Note, however, that teacher responses written in complete sentences model the kind of writing we ask of our students.) Grades for journals can be based on the number, length, and diversity of journal entries.

The writing process, as presented on page 45 and in each chapter thereafter, has four steps: Prewrite, Write, Edit, and Write the Final Draft.

- When they do prewriting, students interact with their classmates in various ways. They brainstorm, take notes, question one another, do freewriting, and learn strategies for organizing ideas. Interaction with classmates is good for generating ideas and, like peer review later on, raises student awareness of the audience for their writing.
- When they write a first draft, students rely on their notes and refer back to the models in the Chapter Preview. This can be done in class or for homework. Composing in class allows you to observe and assist; composing at home saves class time. You may wish to have students hand in both their prewriting and their first draft along with their final draft for clues to the writer's thinking and the development of the paragraph.

- Students must take responsibility for checking and improving their own work. However, they are often best able to do so when they can see their writing through the eyes of a reader and when they develop revising and editing skills by reviewing other writers' work. For these reasons, I encourage peer review but only at a very basic level. Each chapter includes a simple checklist to guide the reviewer through the process slowly and thoughtfully. See page 46 for an example of a peer reviewer's markings on a first draft.
- The term *final draft* is used to mean a revised and edited draft handed in to the teacher, possibly for a grade. It is not necessarily the last draft that the student will write. As explained to the student under Results of the Writing Process, another draft, based on written and/or oral feedback from you, may be required. Also, a useful set of correction symbols can be found in Appendix N, along with sample marked-up paragraphs, which can form the basis of lessons in understanding and responding to teacher feedback.

Students are instructed to hand in new drafts stapled on top of earlier ones so that you can make comparisons. You may wish to have students keep their finals drafts in a folder so that they compile a collection of paragraphs written during the course. They can go back later and further revise their work so that in effect the writing course mirrors the writing process: full of brainstorming, drafting, and sharing early on, with a greater emphasis on polishing later, when students can apply everything they have learned to date about good English sentences and paragraphs.

Answer Key   An Answer Key is available upon request from the publisher.

Acknowledgments

First and foremost, I would like to thank two key people for entrusting me with this project: Laura Le Dréan, Pearson Longman executive editor, and Ann Hogue, author of *First Steps in Academic Writing* and, with Alice Oshima, *Introduction to Academic Writing* and *Writing Academic English*. I would also like to thank all the members of the Longman team whose work helped bring this book to life, particularly Kim Steiner, John Beaumont, Paula Van Ells, and Gina DiLillo.

The following reviewers helped to shape this book with their thoughtful comments and suggestions, for which I thank them: **Gena Bennett**, Georgia State University, Georgia; **Vicki Blaho**, Santa Monica College, California; **Charlotte Calobrisi**, Northern Virginia Community College, Virginia; **Jackye Cumby**, Mercer University, Georgia; **Diana Davidson Del Toro**, Cuyamaca College, California; **Greg Davis**, Portland State University, Oregon; **Diane Harris**, Imperial Valley College, California; **Shelagh Lariviere**, College of the North Atlantic, Doha, Qatar; **Linda Lieberman**, College of Marin, California; **Kathy Llanos**, Cypress College, California; **Theresa Nahim**, Pace University, New York; **Tara Narcross**, Columbus State Community College, Ohio; **Mark Neville**, Alhosn University, Abu Dhabi, UAE; **Daria Ruzicka**; **Christine Tierney**, Houston Community College, Texas; **Lay Kuan Toh**, Westchester Community College, New York; **Stephen Whelan**, College of the North Atlantic, Doha, Qatar.

In addition, I am grateful for the support and feedback provided by my ESL colleagues at Holyoke Community College, Massachusetts: Pam Kennedy, Eileen Kelley, Vivian Leskes, Rubaba Matin, Maggie Sweeney, Judith Roberts, Darcy Sweeney, Tusi Gastonguay, and David Kestenbaum. I would also like to thank the following colleagues and friends for their help: Ismet Ozkilic and Valentyna Semyrog of Holyoke Community College; Mahmoud Arani of St. Michael's College, Vermont; and Craig Butler of Hong Kong International School.

Finally, a special thank you and a round of applause to the students who shared samples of their writing with me, some of which have been adapted for this book: Mary Benvenutty, Wai Chan, Antonio Colon, Blasnelly Diodonet, Leslie Dones, Rose Feliciano Reyes, Juliana Gonzalez, Maryia Hancharonak, Zam Zam Hussein, Nataliya Kondratyuk, Nadia Kravchuk, Iris Laviera, Nelly Martinez, Oksana Morozova, Tam Kenny Nguyen, Mirjeta Nuhiu, Venhar Nuhiu, Moises Ortiz, Tatyana Pchelka, Viktor Rafalskiy, Osmayra Rivera, Ina Ruskevich, Yelena Sokolova, Jason Son, Minja Son, Vera Stolyarova, and Penny Wu.

This book is dedicated to a great teacher of mine, Jane Boggs Sloan. Twenty-five years later, when faced with a teaching dilemma, I still ask myself, "What would Jane do?"

To the Student

Welcome to *Fundamentals of Academic Writing*! Learning to write in English is like learning to play the game of baseball, or almost any sport. There are many rules that all players must follow, but no two games are ever alike. Just as every game is different, so is every piece of writing—and every writer. This book will help you learn the rules that good writers know. It will also give you many chances to "play the game" of writing English. I hope that you will write a lot, that you will have fun writing, and that you will feel proud of your work.

Linda Butler

Your Classmates

Classmates

Prewriting

Ask Questions

Introduce Your Partner

Writing

Look at Model Paragraphs

Write a Paragraph About Your Partner

Sharing

Show Your Paragraph to Your Partner

Share Paragraphs with Your Class

Prewriting

Thinking before writing

Before you write, you need a **topic** — something to write about. Here is a topic for you: a classmate. Write about a person in your class. This classmate will be your **partner** — someone you work with.

Step 1: Work with a partner. Ask your partner these questions. Listen and write the answers. If you cannot spell a word, ask, "How do you spell that?"

1. What's your first name? _____

2. What's your last name? _____

3. Where are you from? _____

4. What's your first language? _____

5. Where do you live? _____

6. Who lives with you? _____

7. Do you have a job? _____

8. What do you like to do in your free time? _____

Martin is asking Yelena about spelling.

Step 2: Are there any extra questions you want to ask? Ask your questions, and write the answers here.

_____

_____

_____

Yelena is introducing Martin.

Step 3: Introduce your partner to the class or to a small group of classmates. Tell three or four facts about your partner.

Writing

You are going to write a paragraph about your partner.

Step 1: Read these two paragraphs.

Martin Herrera

My Classmate Yelena

My classmate Yelena Politova is an interesting person.

Im going to be with my Lau

She is from Ukraine. She speaks Ukrainian and Russian.

I bought a lot of Presents for Anna

She lives with her family in Chicago. She is married. She has

we had so much fun. we stayed their for

one week so we did not to see everything that we

one son and one daughter. She works part-time at the

wanted to see

Chicago Animal Hospital. I hope to learn more about her.

I was holly to see all my family and Friend

Ali Abdi

My Classmate Jason

My classmate Jason Kim is an interesting person. He is

from Seoul, Korea. His first language is Korean. He lives

on campus. He has a roommate. He is not married. He does

not have a job. In his free time, he likes to play soccer and

video games. He loves to sleep.

Step 2: Take a piece of lined paper. Write your name at the top of the paper, on the right. Then write this title:

My Classmate _____
                        (your partner's first name)

Step 3: Write a paragraph about your partner. Follow the examples on page 4. Begin with this sentence:

My classmate _____ is an interesting person.
                        (name)

Sharing

Step 1: Show your paragraph to your partner. Is the information correct? Make changes if necessary.

Step 2: Your teacher may ask the class to share all the paragraphs. Then you can read other paragraphs and learn about people in your class.

Introducing Yourself

Nice to meet you!

Chapter Preview

You are going to write a paragraph about yourself. First, look at three **model paragraphs**. Models are examples. Model sentences and paragraphs help writers. Models help us think about what we want to write.

1. Work with a partner. Read each model paragraph. At the right, circle the information you find in the paragraph.

I would like to introduce myself. My name is Shaukat Matin. My nickname is Salim. I am from Pakistan. I speak Bengali. I am married. I live with my wife and our son. I want to study computers.

(name)	work
home country	classes at school
languages	free-time fun
where he lives	friends
age	plans for the future
family	

I would like to introduce myself. My name is Catherine Ortíz. I am nineteen years old. I am from Honduras. I live on campus. On weekends, I like to go dancing with my boyfriend. I love music, especially Latin music.

name	work
home country	classes at school
languages	free-time fun
where she lives	friends
age	plans for the future
family	

I would like to introduce myself. My name is Michelle André. I am a new student. I am taking writing, reading, and oral communication. My mother and father and sister are in Haiti. I miss my family. I live with my aunt. I work part-time in her restaurant.

name	work
home country	classes at school
languages	free-time fun
where she lives	friends
age	plans for the future
family	

2. Write six or more sentences about yourself. Look at the three model paragraphs for help.

1. My name is _____

2. I am from _____

3. I speak _____

4. _____

5. _____

6. _____

_____

_____

3. Show your sentences to your partner. Read your partner's sentences. Do you understand all your partner's sentences? Tell your partner if something is not clear.

You will use your sentences later in this chapter to write a paragraph about yourself (page 11).

PART 1 | Organization

From Words to Sentences to Paragraphs

We use **letters** to form **words**.

	Letters
Capital Letters	A B C D E....
Small Letters	a b c d e....

→

Words
hi
love
students
Los Angeles
ice cream

We use words to form **sentences**.

Sentences
I am a student. This is my book. What's your name? Do you like pizza?

We use sentences to form **paragraphs**. A paragraph is a group of sentences about one topic.

Read this paragraph.

Strawberries are a delicious kind of fruit. They are small and red. They are sweet and juicy. I have strawberries in my garden every summer. I love to eat them.

The topic of this paragraph is _____

What Does a Paragraph Look Like?

The same paragraph about strawberries is below. Look at these two things:

(1) The first sentence is **indented**. There is a space before it. Remember to indent the first sentence in your paragraphs.

(2) The second sentence follows the first sentence on the same line. It does not go on a new line.

NEW SENTENCE, SAME LINE

INDENT

→Strawberries are a delicious kind of fruit. They are small and red. They are sweet and juicy. I have strawberries in my garden every summer. I love to eat them.

Work alone or with a partner. Read the letter. Answer the questions below.

$\mathcal{N}$

September 4

Dear Ms. Kennedy,

My name is Nadia Duric. I am a new student. I am in your Writing 1 class. I want to tell you a little about myself.

My family is from Kosovo. I live with my parents, my two little brothers, and my cousin. We have an apartment in Middletown.

This is my first week of school. I am happy to be here. I want to learn English very much. I want to finish college and get a good job.

Sincerely yours,

Nadia Duric

1. How many paragraphs are there in Nadia's letter? _____

2. What is the topic of the second paragraph? _____

Copy the sentences below to complete the paragraph on page 11. Continue skipping lines.

There are two main points about paragraphs.

First, all the sentences in a paragraph are about one topic.

Second, a paragraph has a special format.

The first sentence is indented.

The next sentence starts right after the first one.

These are important things to remember about paragraphs.

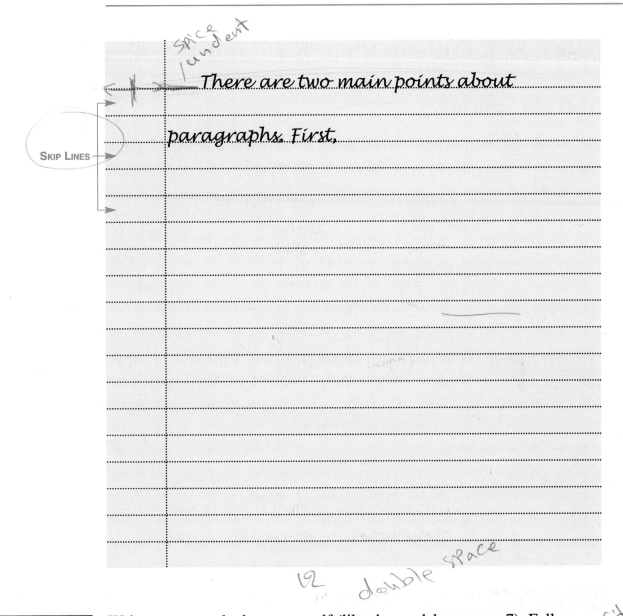

space/indent

There are two main points about

SKIP LINES →

paragraphs. First,

double space

PRACTICE 1.3

Writing a Paragraph About Yourself

Write a paragraph about yourself (like the models on page 7). Follow these steps.

Step 1: Take a piece of paper. Write your name at the top.

Step 2: Indent and begin your paragraph with this sentence:

I would like to introduce myself.

Step 3: Look at the sentences you wrote on page 8. Change your sentences if you want.

Step 4: Complete your paragraph by copying your sentences. Skip lines.

PART 2 | Sentence Structure and Mechanics

What Is a Sentence?

A sentence is a group of words that expresses a complete idea. A sentence always has a **subject** and a **verb**.

Look at the subjects and verbs in these sentences.

SUBJECT VERB
Hiro (plays) the guitar.

SUBJECT VERB
He (loves) music.

PRACTICE 1.4

Subjects and Verbs

Work alone or with a partner. Circle the verb in each sentence. Write *V* above it. Then underline the subject of that verb. Write *S* above it.

     S   V

1. Ahmet (drives) a taxi.

2. Lucia rides the bus.

3. Mr. Parker speaks English.

4. A photographer takes pictures.

5. Fish swim in the ocean.

6. The sun sets in the evening.

7. I drink tea.

8. We go to the mall on Saturdays.

9. My friends watch soccer on TV.

10. Chocolate tastes good.

What Does a Sentence Look Like?

There are different kinds of sentences. Some sentences are **statements**, and some sentences are **questions**. Look at these examples with your class. How are statements and questions the same? How are they different?

Sentences

Statements	Questions
I am from Colombia.	Where are you from?
My name is Maria.	What is your name?
I am a new student.	Are you a new student?
My first language is Spanish.	Do you speak Spanish?

Sentences need **capital letters** and **punctuation**. Every sentence begins with a capital letter. Every sentence has a punctuation mark at the end.

Rules	Examples
1. Use a capital letter for the first word in a sentence.	T the class is in room 342.
2. Put a period (.) after a statement.	This sentence is a statement.
3. Put a question mark (?) after a question.	Do you have any questions?

PRACTICE 1.5

Using Capital Letters and End Punctuation

Work alone or with a partner. Add a capital letter to each sentence. Put a period after each statement. Put a question mark after each question.

A
1. are you married?

2. my friend speaks English

3. are you from China

4. he is from Mexico

5. do you drink coffee

6. the movie starts at 7:00

7. where do you live

8. how do you spell your name

9. she works part-time

10. we like to go dancing

PRACTICE 1.6

Word Order:
Statements

Work alone or with a partner. Put the words in order. Write statements. Look at the examples of statements on page 13 for help. Add periods.

1. is / My class / big   <u>My class is big.</u>

2. 24 classmates / have / I _____

3. from many countries / come / We _____

4. friendly / My classmates / are _____

5. Ms. Green / is / The teacher's name _____

6. We / in room 245 / meet _____

7. from / I / China / am _____

8. language / first / is / My / Chinese _____

PRACTICE 1.7

Word Order:
Questions

Work alone or with a partner. Put the words in order. Write questions. Look at the examples of questions on page 13 for help. Add question marks.

1. that man / Who is   <u>Who is that man?</u>

2. his first name / What is _____

3. is / What / last name / his _____

4. he / Is / a new student _____

5. in this class / he / Is _____

6. he / Does / English / speak _____

7. from / is / he / Where _____

8. is / he / How old _____

PRACTICE 1.8

Editing: Capital Letters

Some sentences are missing capital letters on the first word. Make corrections.

       M

~~my~~ name is Mayra. I am from the Dominican Republic. my first language is Spanish. now I live in Hartford. today is my first day in this school. I want to learn English. it is very important for my future.

PRACTICE 1.9

Editing: Capital Letters and Periods

Make corrections to this paragraph. Add five more capital letters and seven more periods.

                                  S

Kazumi is one of my classmates. ~~$~~he is from Japan she speaks Japanese her parents live in Tokyo she has no brothers or sisters she is single Kazumi likes music and fashion her clothes are beautiful

PRACTICE 1.10

Writing a Paragraph About Your Class

A. Complete the information about your class.

    Example: 1. I am taking __English 10._____
                                     (course name / number)

        2. My class meets on __Monday, Wednesday, and Friday._____
                                    (day or days)

        3. It meets from __9:30 A.M._____ to __11:45 A.M.____
                      (start time)   (end time)

1. I am taking _____
                            (course name / number)

2. My class meets on _____
                                 (day or days)

3. It meets from _____ to _____
                  (start time)   (end time)

4. We meet in _____
                            (room number)

5. Our teacher's name is _____
                              (name)

6. The work is _____
                       (easy / hard / interesting)

B. Copy the sentences from Part A on the lines below. Write them as a paragraph.

_____I am taking_____

_____

_____

_____

_____

_____

PART 3 | Grammar and Vocabulary

Verbs

On page 12, you learned about sentences. Remember, every sentence needs a verb. The **boldfaced** parts of these sentences are verbs:

They **live** in Egypt.

He **speaks** Japanese.

I'**m** in this class.

Where'**s** room 250?

Many verbs are words for actions. They are words for things that someone or something does, like *builds, drives,* or *plays.* These verbs describe movement or change that you can see. In the next three pictures, you can see what Arturo does.

Arturo **builds** houses.

He **drives** a sports car.

He **plays** baseball.

Other verbs do not express actions. We cannot see any movement or change. Examples of these verbs are *is*, *likes*, and *has*. In the next pictures, you cannot see Arturo do anything.

Arturo **is** happy.

He **likes** his job.

He **has** many friends.

PRACTICE 1.11

Recognizing Verbs

Work alone or with a partner. Circle the verb in each sentence.

1. I (have) a cell phone.

2. I make a lot of phone calls.

3. My friends call me, too.

4. We talk a lot.

5. Sometimes they leave messages.

6. I listen to my messages.

7. My phone takes pictures, too.

8. It is very important to me.

PRACTICE 1.12

*Building
Sentences with
Common Verbs*

Work with a partner. Write six statements. Use words from each box.
Use all six verbs.

Subject	Verb	
my roommate my friend he she	is rides has eats listens goes	a cell phone a computer a student fish horses the bus to music to movies

Example: My roommate has a cell phone.

1. _____

2. _____

3. _____

4. _____

5. _____

6. _____

PRACTICE 1.13

*Placing Verbs
in Statements*

Work alone or with a partner. Add the verb in parentheses to the right
place in the statement.

Example: (is) This ∧ Dao. *is*

1. (is) Dao my friend.

2. (is) She from Thailand.

3. (means) Her name "stars" in Thai.

4. (likes) Dao to cook.

5. (cooks) She Thai food.

6. (go) We to the Asian market together.

7. (buys) She vegetables, tofu, and
   lemongrass.

8. (makes) She dinner for us.

9. (tastes) Everything delicious!

Nouns

A **noun** is a word for a person, place, thing, or idea.

Look at the chart. The **boldfaced** words are nouns.

	What does the noun name?			
	a person	a place	a thing	an idea
1. I love my **brother**.	x			
2. The **singer** is smiling.	x			
3. Do you know **Marta**?	x			
4. He is at the **airport**.		x		
5. The **library** is open today.		x		
6. They live in **Saudi Arabia**.		x		
7. Would you like some **ice cream**?			x	
8. That **watch** is expensive.			x	
9. He drives a **Toyota**.			x	
10. **Education** is important to me.				x
11. I have **fun** with my friends.				x
12. What **time** is it?				x

PRACTICE 1.14

Identifying Meanings of Nouns

Work alone or with a partner. Look at the fifteen **boldfaced** nouns in this paragraph. Write *person*, *place*, *thing*, or *idea* above each noun. (*Note*: For some nouns, there can be more than one answer.)

        place   thing/place

New York City is my favorite **city**. I have several **relatives** in New York. My

aunt and **uncle** live there, and my **sister** does, too. She has an **apartment** near

Central Park. I like to spend **time** with her. We go to **clubs** to listen to **music**.

We go out to eat together. She shows me **stores** with **clothes** at great **prices**.

I always have **fun** in New York.

PRACTICE 1.15

Building Vocabulary: Nouns

Work with a partner or in a small group. Write as many nouns as you can. Count your nouns, and write the total.

1. Nouns for people in a family:

   Examples: mother, father

   _____

   _____

   _____ Total: _____

2. Nouns for things inside a house:

   _____

   _____

   _____ Total: _____

3. Nouns for places to go in a city:

   _____

   _____

   _____ Total: _____

Singular and Plural Nouns

Most nouns have **singular** and **plural** forms. *Singular* means "only one." *Plural* means "more than one." Plural nouns usually end in -*s*.

Singular	Plural
hot dog	hot dog**s**
watch	watch**es**
library	librar**ies**

See Appendix C for spelling rules for plural nouns.

Some plural nouns are **irregular**. They do not follow the rules for plural nouns. They do not end in -*s*.

Singular	Plural
person	people
man	men
woman	women
child	children

See Appendix C for more irregular plural nouns.

PRACTICE 1.16

Writing Plural Nouns

Write the plural form of each singular noun. (See Appendix C for help with spelling.)

1. pencil _____pencils_____   7. dish _____

2. day _____   8. dictionary _____

3. city _____   9. family _____

4. box _____   10. glass _____

5. child _____   11. man _____

6. person _____   12. woman _____

PRACTICE 1.17

*Identifying
Singular Versus
Plural Nouns*

Look at the **boldfaced** nouns in this paragraph. Mark each noun *s* (singular) or *pl* (plural).

                  s

    Paris is the **capital** of France. It is a beautiful **city**. Millions of **people** visit Paris each **year**. There are wonderful **museums**, historic **buildings**, lovely **parks**, and excellent **restaurants**. A **visitor** can have a great **time** in Paris.

The river Seine in Paris

PRACTICE 1.18

*Recognizing
Nouns*

Circle the fourteen nouns in this paragraph. The first noun is circled for you. Mark each noun *s* (singular) or *pl* (plural).

         pl

(Dolphins) are interesting animals. First, a dolphin is not a fish. It is a mammal, like cats, horses, and people. Also, did you know that a dolphin sleeps with one eye open? One half of the dolphin's brain rests, and the other half stays awake.

A bottlenose dolphin

PRACTICE 1.19

*Building
Vocabulary:
Nouns
and Verbs*

Work with a partner. Complete the chart with nouns and verbs. Write two words in each box. Each word must begin with the letter at the top.

	A	**B**	**C**	**D**	**E**
Nouns	apple Alberto				
Verbs	ask answer				

PART 4 | The Writing Process

What Is a Process?

A **process** is a series of **steps** or actions. You take these steps because you want to reach a **goal**. The steps in the process will help you get the **results** you want.

In your everyday life, you often follow a process. For example, you follow a process when you wash clothes in a washing machine. Your goal is to get your clothes clean. What do you do first? What do you do next? Number these steps in order from 1 to 5.

Step ___ : Take the clothes out of the machine.

Step _1_ : Put the clothes into the machine.

Step ___ : Add detergent.

Step ___ : Wait for the machine to finish.

Step ___ : Start the machine.

What is the result of this process? Clean clothes!

Writers also follow a process. The writing process can help you write clear and correct paragraphs in English. The writing process looks something like this:

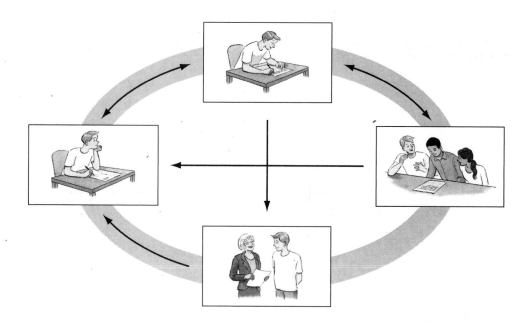

Look at the picture of the writing process on page 23, and discuss these questions with your class:

- Where does the writing process begin?
- What is the next step?
- How does the process continue?
- What happens after the teacher returns a paper to a student?

PRACTICE 1.20

Understanding Key Words

Complete the sentences. Use the same word from the box in sentences *a* and *b*.

goal	process	result	step

1. (a) A _____*goal*_____ is something you want to do or to have in the future.

   (b) For example, the _____*goal*_____ of a medical student is to become a doctor.

2. (a) A _____ is something that happens or exists because of something else.

   (b) If you mix the colors blue and yellow, the _____ is green.

3. (a) A _____ is one action in a series of actions. You take these actions to solve a problem or to get to a result.

   (b) For example, you can make a phone call in two easy _____s: (1) Pick up the receiver. (2) Press the numbers.

4. (a) A _____ is a series of actions you do or steps you take to get a result.

   (b) In this book, you will learn the steps of the writing _____.

Expansion Activities

Keeping a Journal

Writing in a **journal** can help you become a better writer in English. A journal is a notebook in which you write about your life.

Each time you write in your journal, you make a **journal entry**. Sometimes your journal entries will be short. Sometimes you will want to write more.

Your teacher will read your journal and write back to you in it. Your journal is like a conversation between you and your teacher. In your journal, you can ask your teacher questions. Your teacher can ask you questions, too. Then you should write the answers or talk to your teacher.

Your journal writing will be different from the other writing you do for this class. You will not need to correct your journal entries.

Frequently Asked Questions (FAQs) About Journals

1. What should I write about?

   You can write about things that happen in your life or things you are thinking about. You will also find ideas for journal entries in this book.

2. Who decides on the topic for a journal entry?

   Sometimes your teacher will give you a topic. Sometimes you can choose your own topic.

3. Who will read my journal?

   Your teacher will. You can share it with friends and classmates, too, if you want.

4. How often should I write journal entries? How often will the teacher read them?

   Ask your teacher.

---

spend
I spend my

Look at this example of an entry in Murat's journal and the teacher's comments.

April 26

Soccer is my favorite sport. I played soccer at my high school. Now I play with friends every day at 4:30 or 5:00 P.M. We play near the dining hall. Sometimes we have six or seven players, sometimes fifteen or twenty. We don't have real games. We play for fun.

Great! I'm glad you have a chance to play your sport. Do you ever watch soccer on TV?

This is called "playing pick-up" (when you play with anyone who comes).

---

1. Get a notebook to use for your journal.

   Remember to:

   a. Put the date before each journal entry.

   b. Leave margins on the left and right side of each page. Leave some space after each journal entry, too. Your teacher will need space in your journal to write back to you.

2. For your first journal entry, write about yourself. What do you want your teacher to know about you? What is important in your life?

3. Here are some ideas for more journal entries:

   • Describe your family. Give your family members' names and ages, and tell something about them.
   • Do you like music? What kind of music do you listen to? When and where do you listen to music?
   • Write about someone you know at school. What is this person's name? Where is he or she from? What do you know about this person?
   • Write about this class or the school. Do you have any questions for your teacher?

Describing Your Morning Routine

It's time to get ready for the day.

Chapter Preview

Part 1: Organization
What Should Your Paper Look Like?
Papers Typed on a Computer

Part 2: Grammar and Sentence Structure
Subject Pronouns
The Simple Present of *Be*
Basic Sentence Patterns with *Be*

Part 3: Mechanics
Rules for Capitalization

Part 4: The Writing Process
The Steps in the Writing Process
Your Paragraph: *Getting Ready for the Day*
Results of the Writing Process

Expansion Activities

Chapter Preview

Work with a partner or in a small group. Read the model paragraphs. Each paragraph describes someone's morning **routine** — the things they usually do. Answer the questions that follow. *[handwritten: simple present tense]*

MODEL

Paragraph 1

> **My Morning Routine**
>
> It is easy for me to get ready for the day. I get up at 8:30 A.M. I wash my face and brush my teeth. I put on my clothes. Then I put my books in my backpack. I leave my room at 8:45 A.M. I walk to Kerry Hall. My first class is from 9:00 to 9:50 A.M. After class, I am very hungry. I go to the dining hall for a big breakfast. That is my morning routine.

MODEL

Paragraph 2

> **Getting Ready for the Day**
>
> I do many things to get ready for the day. I get up at 6:30 A.M. First, I take a shower. Then I get dressed, fix my hair, and put on my makeup. At 7:15 A.M., I wake up my husband and my children. I help my children get dressed. Then we have breakfast. At 8:00 A.M., I walk my daughter to the bus for school. After that, I drive my son to day care. Finally, I go to school for my 9:00 A.M. class. That is my busy morning routine. *[handwritten: I get my books and supplies ready]*

[handwritten: 12-15-]

Questions about model paragraph 1:

1. What is the topic of the paragraph? _____
   [handwritten: Grammer]

2. Which word describes the writer's morning routine? Circle it:
   (busy / easy / hungry)

3. How much time does the writer need before class each day?

   _____

4. Where do you think the writer lives? _____

[handwritten: my whole]

5. Write the verbs the writer uses:

a. It _____ easy for me to get ready for the day.

b. I _____ at 8:30 A.M.

c. I _____ my clothes.

d. My first class _____ from 9:00 to 9:50 A.M.

e. After class, I _____ very hungry.

f. That _____ my morning routine.

6. Write the words the writer uses to show time:

a. I get up _____ 8:30 A.M.

b. My first class is _____ 9:00 _____ 9:50 A.M.

c. _____ class, I am very hungry.

Questions about model paragraph 2:

1. What is the topic of the paragraph? _____

2. What word describes the morning routine of this writer? _____

3. How much time does the writer need before class each day?

_____

4. Talk about the writer's morning routine. What is the same for her and the writer of paragraph 1? What is different?

5. Write the verbs the writer uses:

a. First, I _____ a shower.

b. Then I _____ dressed, _____ my hair, and _____ my makeup.

c. At 7:15 A.M., I _____ my husband and my children.

d. Then we _____ breakfast.

6. Write the words the writer uses to show the order of her actions:

a. _____ , I take a shower.

b. _____ I get dressed, fix my hair, and put on my makeup.

c. _____ , I drive my son to day care.

d. _____ , I go to school for my 9:00 A.M. class.

You will write a paragraph about your morning routine later in this chapter (page 48).

PART 1 | Organization

What Should Your Paper Look Like?

You will write many paragraphs for this class. When you write a paragraph, you need to think about the **format** of your paper — the way it looks.

1. The paper

Use lined paper. Notebook paper that is 8½ by 11 inches is a good size.

2. The heading

The heading goes in the upper right-hand corner of your paper. The heading includes your name and the date. Your teacher may ask you to add other information, too.

3. The title

A title tells the topic of your paragraph. A title is not a sentence. It is just a few words or even one word only. Your title goes on the top line, in the middle.

4. Skipping lines

Do not write on the line below your title. Skip that line. Begin writing on the third line. Continue skipping lines.

5. **Margins**

Leave spaces on the left and right sides of your paper. These spaces are the margins.

6. **Keeping words together**

Sometimes a word is too long. It cannot fit at the end of a line. Do not divide the word into two parts. Move the whole word to the beginning of the next line.

Your paper should look like this:

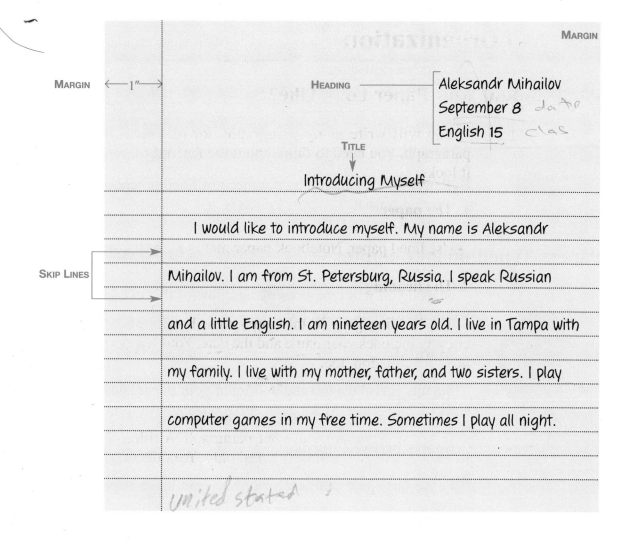

<table>
<tr><td>

PRACTICE 2.1

Errors in Format

</td><td>

A. Work alone or with a partner. Look at Vu's paper. How many problems can you find in the format of his paper? Mark them with circles or arrows.

</td></tr>
</table>

I wake up every mor... Introducing Myself
I Am. bruch

I would like to introduce myself. My name is Vu Le. I am from Ho Chi

Minh City in Viet Nam. I speak Vietnamese and English.

I live with my aunt, my uncle, and my cousins. I am not married.

I am twenty years old.

I like good food. I like to cook. In the future, I want to open a Viet-

namese restaurant.

Vu Le

B. Rewrite Vu's paragraph on a piece of lined notebook paper. Use the correct format.

Papers Typed on a Computer

Maybe you will type your paragraphs for this class on a computer. You will need to think about the format of your paper.

1. Margins

Set margins at the top and bottom of your paper and on the left and right sides of your paper. Make them about one inch (or three centimeters) wide.

2. Spaces between words

Leave one space after each word. Do not leave a space before a period.

Do this: Do not do this:

| This spacing is correct. |

| T his spacing isnot correct . |

3. Spaces between lines

Double-space your paragraph.

Do this:

Do not do this:

These sentences are **double-spaced**. There is space between the lines for corrections. Your paper should look like this.

These sentences are **single-spaced**. There is very little space between the lines. There is not enough space to write corrections.

4. Saving your work

Remember to save your work. You can use your paragraph title as the file name. Add the date. For example, write *Myself 10102007*. Make a backup copy of the file.

PRACTICE 2.2

Different Formats

A. Look at the formats of Deko's paper and Marissa's e-mail message. Both examples were typed on a computer, and both are correct.

Deko Hussein
English 11B
November 12

My Computer

My computer is helpful. I use it for school. I write papers on my computer. I print my papers on my printer. I also use my computer to write to my family and friends. I send e-mail.

I use my computer for the Internet, too. I find information online. I am glad to have a computer.

> **From:** mldavis@nycc.ny.us
> **To:** jwashin@statecoll.edu
> **Sent:** Monday, September 18, 23:07
> **Subject:** helloooooo
>
> Hi Jen
>
> How are you? I'm pretty good. School is OK so far. My teachers are nice. I have friends in all my classes.
>
> My roommate is nice. Her name is Parinda. She is from Thailand. She speaks English really well.
>
> I have a new cell phone number. It's (210) 555-1234. Call me! But not before 10:00 A.M. please. :–)
>
> Marissa

B. Work with a partner or in a small group. Look at headings, titles, spacing, margins, and indenting in the two examples. Talk about what is the same and what is different.

PART 2 | Grammar and Sentence Structure

Subject Pronouns

In Chapter 1, you learned about nouns. Remember, a noun is a word for a person, place, thing, or idea. Pronouns can take the place of nouns. A **subject pronoun** can be the subject of a sentence.

Subject Pronouns

Singular	Plural
I	we
you	you
he	
she	they
it	

Study these rules and examples.

Rules	Examples
1. Subject pronouns can take the place of subject nouns.	Lucia is from Brazil. ~~Lucia~~ ^She^ speaks Portuguese.
2. Use a noun or a subject pronoun, not both.	Your <u>friend</u> is nice. <u>He</u> is nice. Not: Your friend ~~he~~ is nice.
3. Use *they* to refer to people or things.	The <u>children</u> are small. **They** are two years old. The <u>cars</u> are not new. **They** are two years old.
4. Use *it* to tell: the time the day the date the weather	It is nine o'clock (9:00). It is Wednesday. It is September 25. It is warm and sunny.

PRACTICE 2.3

Using Subject Pronouns

Complete each sentence with the correct subject pronoun.

1. That man's name is Hugo. ____He____ is from Mali.

2. My name is Nanami. _____ am from Osaka.

3. What day is it today? _____ is Thursday.

4. I know that girl. _____ is in my class.

5. The weather is nice. _____ is cool.

6. These are good cookies. _____ are delicious.

7. My brothers can sing. _____ are good singers.

8. What time is it? _____ is 4:30 P.M.

9. You and I need to work together. _____ are partners.

10. Please call me. _____ and I need to talk.

PRACTICE 2.4

Editing: Errors with Subject Pronouns

Work alone or with a partner. Correct the subject pronoun error in each sentence.

1. Martin he has a motorcycle.

2. You and i have the same teachers.

3. Is Friday.

4. He is a nice girl.

5. My friends they are at the mall.

6. She is a little boy.

7. They is two o'clock.

8. Is hot today.

The Simple Present of *Be*

The words *am, is*, and *are* are verbs. They are the **simple present** forms of the verb *be*. *Be* is the **base form** of the verb.

Affirmative Statements with *Be*

Singular		
Subject	***Be***	
I	**am**	
You	**are**	
He		
She	**is**	in class.
It		
Bill		

Plural		
Subject	***Be***	
We		
You		
They	**are**	in class.
Bill and Al		

See Appendix D for contractions with be.

PRACTICE 2.5

Be in Affirmative Statements

Complete the statements. Use the correct form of the verb *be*.

1. This exercise ____is____ easy.

2. I _____ busy.

3. That is my sister. She _____ sixteen years old.

4. My friend _____ from Lebanon.

5. Many people _____ in the lab.

6. You _____ my partner.

7. I have two brothers. They _____ at home.

8. We _____ on page 37.

9. You and I _____ in the same group.

10. My morning routine ____ _____ simple.

Negative Statements with *Be*

Singular			
Subject	*Be*	*Not*	
I	am		
You	are		
He		not	in class.
She	is		
It			
Bill			

Plural			
Subject	*Be*	*Not*	
We			
You			
They	are	not	in class.
Bill and Al			

See Appendix D for contractions with be.

PRACTICE 2.6

Be in Negative Statements

Complete the statements. Use the correct form of the verb *be* + *not*.

1. You __are not__ late.

2. The exercises _____ difficult.

3. It _____ cold today.

4. Omar _____ here.

5. The teacher _____ in his office.

6. That is my sister. She _____ a student.

7. You and Marta _____ new students.

8. I _____ in your class.

9. I have a brother. He _____ married.

10. We _____ ready.

PRACTICE 2.7

Complete Sentences with Be

Look at each group of words. Check (✓) **It is a complete sentence.** or **It is not a sentence. There is no verb.** Then correct the incomplete sentences.

	It is a complete sentence.	It is not a sentence. There is no verb.
1. I *am* from Kuwait.		✓
2. What is your name?		
3. We *are* partners.		✓
4. Halima is my sister.		
5. I *am* twenty-two years old.		✓
6. My father and my mother *are* in Nepal.		✓
7. Ms. Kelley is my teacher.		
8. How old are you?		
9. The students *are* in the classroom.		
10. Javier *is* tall and handsome.		

PRACTICE 2.8

Editing: Statements with Be

Work alone or with a partner. Look at each statement. Check (✓) *Correct* or *Incorrect*. Make corrections.

Correct	Incorrect	
☐	☑	1. He ~~no~~ *not* is in class today.
☑	☐	2. I am a student.
☐	☑	3. We not at home.
☐	☑	4. It a nice day.
☐	☑	5. The teacher *is not* ~~no~~ is here.
☐	☑	6. You in class.
☑	☐	7. Hana is not a new student.
☐	☑	8. I am no cold.
☐	☑	9. Mr. Sweeney a teacher.
☐	☑	10. I busy in the morning.

Basic Sentence Patterns with *Be*

The verb *be* has many uses. Here are three ways to use *be* in sentences:

Rules	Examples	
1. To identify a person or thing: Use *be* + a noun.	**Subject**	**Be + Noun**
	They	**are** my <u>friends</u>.
	Dolphins	**are** <u>mammals</u>.
	Mali	**is** a <u>country</u> in Africa.
2. To tell where someone or something is: Use *be* + an expression of place.	**Subject**	**Be + Expression of Place**
	My house	**is** <u>on Park Street</u>.
	The students	**are** <u>in room 152</u>.
	I	**am** <u>here</u>.
3. To describe someone or something: Use *be* + an adjective or age.	**Subject**	**Be + Adjective/Age**
	The sky	**is** <u>blue</u>.
	They	**are** <u>married</u>.
	I	**am** <u>twenty years old</u>.

The verbs *am, is*, and *are* can be used with verbs ending in *-ing*:

Shhh! The baby **is** sleep**ing**.
They **are** work**ing** today.

These sentences have **present progressive** verbs. See page 105 for more information.

H. W

PRACTICE 2.9

Sentence Patterns with Be

Work alone or with a partner. Check (✓) the use of the verb *be* in each of these statements.

	Be + Noun	Be + Expression of Place	Be + Adjective/ Age
1. Soccer is a game.	✓		
2. He is seventeen years old.			✓
3. My friends are at the movies.		✓	
4. That is my book.			
5. My eyes are brown.			
6. Her parents are in Costa Rica.			
7. I am not at home.			
8. The movie is at the Central Cinema.			
9. Green beans are vegetables.			
10. I am twenty-four years old.			
11. My brothers are doctors.			
12. Manuel is married.			

PRACTICE 2.10

Statements with **Be**

Edgar is writing about himself and his school. Complete Edgar's statements with a subject from the box and *am, is,* or *are*.

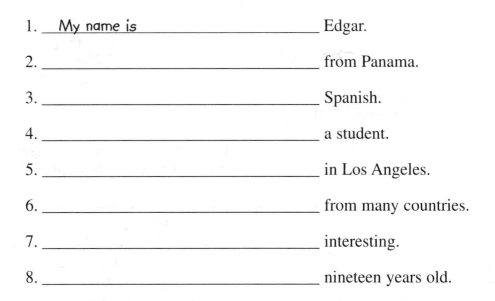

Subjects
My name
I
My first language
My school
My classmates
My classes

1. ___My name is_____ Edgar.

2. _____ from Panama.

3. _____ Spanish.

4. _____ a student.

5. _____ in Los Angeles.

6. _____ from many countries.

7. _____ interesting.

8. _____ nineteen years old.

PRACTICE 2.11

Writing Statements with **Be**

Take a piece of paper. Write ten statements with *be* about yourself and your school. See Practice 2.10 for models. Use all three sentence patterns: *be* + a noun, *be* + an expression of place, and *be* + an adjective/age.

PRACTICE 2.12

Statements with **Be**

Take a piece of paper. Write answers to these questions. Use the verb *be*.

Examples: What day is after Monday?
           Tuesday is after Monday.

           What are carrots and potatoes?
           Carrots and potatoes are vegetables.

1. What day is before Saturday?

2. What day is after Saturday?

3. Where is your teacher from?

4. Where are Brazil and Chile?

5. Where is Canada?

6. What are January and February?

7. What are the Amazon and the Nile?

8. What color are your eyes?

9. What are the colors of your country's flag?

10. How old is your best friend?

PART 3 | Mechanics

Rules for Capitalization

Some words in English must begin with a capital letter. English has many rules for using capital letters. Here are five rules you need to know.

Rules	Examples	
1. Capitalize the subject pronoun *I*.	Now **I** live in Oakland. Rosa and **I** are in the same class.	
2. Capitalize the first letter of a sentence.	**H**is first name is David. **W**hat is his last name?	
3. Capitalize people's names and titles.	My dentist's name is **Dr. Parker**. You can ask **Ms. Evans**.	
4. Capitalize words for nationalities and languages.	**Nationalities**	**Languages**
	Mexican **C**anadian **K**uwaiti	**S**panish **E**nglish **A**rabic
5. Capitalize place names.	She comes from the **United States**. Do you live on **Maxwell Avenue**?	

PRACTICE 2.13

Editing:
Errors in
Capitalization

Correct the fourteen errors in capitalization in this paragraph. The first error is corrected for you.

> I have a friend named thomas. i go to school with him. he speaks chinese and a little english. he is from taiwan. now he is living with his brother. they have an apartment on harvard avenue in brookline, massachusetts.

PRACTICE 2.14

Capitalization

Work alone or with a partner. Review the capitalization rules on page 43. Then write two sample sentences for each rule.

Example: Rule 4:   Mauricio speaks Portuguese and English.

1. Rule 1: _____

_____

2. Rule 2: _____

_____

3. Rule 3: _____

_____

4. Rule 4: _____

_____

5. Rule 5: _____

_____

PART 4 | The Writing Process

The Steps in the Writing Process

On page 23, you learned about the writing process. There are four basic steps in the process:

| Prewrite | Write | Edit | Write the Final Draft |

Step 1: Prewrite

At this step, you begin to get ideas for your paragraph. There are many ways to get ideas, such as brainstorming and freewriting. You will learn about these two ways and other prewriting activities in this book.

Step 2: Write

The first time that you write a paragraph, your paper is called your **first draft**. Your work is not finished! Writing the first draft is only one step on the way to your final paper.

Step 3: Edit

Editing is an important part of the writing process. Editing means checking for mistakes and making corrections. You can also make changes to the **content** — the ideas and information in your paragraph. For example, you can add new information or move sentences. Always edit your writing before you show it to a classmate or to your teacher.

Writer's Tip

When you check for mistakes, read slowly. Sometimes using a ruler (or a piece of paper) can help. Place it under the line you are checking. Move the ruler down as you read. Look at your paragraph word by word, one line at a time.

Sometimes you will do **peer review**. Your classmates are your peers. When you do peer review, you work with a partner. You read and talk about each other's paragraphs. You think about these things:

- the content
- the words and sentences
- the format of the paper

Then you give your partner **feedback** — you say what you think about his or her work. When you give feedback, it is important to be both honest and kind.

Step 4: Write the Final Draft

Sometimes a writer's first draft needs no changes. This does not happen often. Most of the time, writers must write new drafts.

Sometimes your first draft will need only small changes. Then maybe you can erase and make changes on that same paper. Most of the time, you will need to prepare a final draft on a new piece of paper. You will give your final draft to your teacher.

PRACTICE 2.15
Comparing First and Final Drafts

A. Work alone or with a partner. Look at Henry's first draft below. Henry showed his first draft to a classmate. His classmate gave him feedback.

Henry Liu

date   English 112-01

title   margin

→ It easy for me to get ready for the day. My alarm clock

wakes me up at 7:30.

take?

I get up and have a shower. I get dressed. I drive to

school at 8:15. I go to the cafeteria. I very hungry in the morn-

sp?

ing. I eat cereal, fruit, eggs, and toast. I drink orange juice and

tea. I go to my class at 9:00. that is my morning routine.

B. Henry edited his paragraph. Look at his final draft below. What is different? Mark the changes. How many changes did Henry make?

Henry Liu
February 1
English 112-01

Getting Ready for the Day

It is easy for me to get ready for the day. My alarm

clock wakes me up at 7:30. I get up and take a shower.

Then I get dressed. I drive to school at 8:15. First, I go

to the cafeteria. I am very hungry in the morning. I eat

cereal, fruit, eggs, and toast. I drink orange juice and tea.

I talk with my friends. Finally, I go to my class at 9:00.

That is my morning routine.

PRACTICE 2.16

Understanding the Steps in the Writing Process

Work alone or with a partner. Write the words from the box next to their meanings.

editing	first draft	prewriting
feedback	peer review	

1. ____prewriting____ : getting ideas before you start writing

2. _____ : the paper with your first try at writing a paragraph

3. _____ : checking for mistakes and correcting them

4. _____ : working with a partner, looking at each other's writing

5. _____ : the things you tell a writer about his or her paragraph

Your Paragraph: *Getting Ready for the Day*

You are going to write a paragraph about your morning routine.

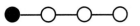

Step 1: Prewrite

a. Take a piece of paper. Make a list of the things you do in the morning to get ready for the day. Begin with the time you get up. Do not write complete sentences. Just **take notes** — write a few words. For example:

> 7:00 A.M. get up
> make tea
> shower, shampoo

b. Work with a partner. Ask your partner, "What do you do in the morning?" Take turns describing your morning routines. Try to use these words: *first, then, after that,* and *finally.*

Step 2: Write

a. Choose a title for your paragraph. You can use *Getting Ready for the Day* or *My Morning Routine* if you like.

b. Begin your paragraph with a general statement about your morning routine. Look at the models on page 28 for examples.

c. Continue your paragraph, using your notes from **Step 1**.

Step 3: Edit

a. Read your paragraph again. It may help you to read it out loud. Make changes if needed.

b. Edit your paper carefully. Check for mistakes before you show it to anyone.

c. Peer review: Exchange papers with a partner. Follow the Reviewer's Checklist below. Check (✓) each box when you finish that step.

Reviewer's Checklist — Chapter 2

Your partner's name: _____

<u>Content</u>

☐ Read all of your partner's paragraph.

☐ Underline any part of the paragraph you do not understand. Ask your partner to explain it.

☐ Ask questions if you want more information about your partner's morning routine.

<u>Form</u>

Look at these parts of your partner's paper. Mark any problems on the paper in pencil. Put a question mark (?) if you are not sure about something. (See Henry Liu's first draft on page 46 for an example of how to mark a paper.)

☐ the heading   ☐ skipping lines

☐ the title   ☐ correct use of capital letters

☐ indenting the first sentence   ☐ a period after every statement

d. Return your partner's paper. Say something nice about it, such as "It's a good start" or "Your paragraph is interesting."

e. Look at your own paper. If you do not agree with a comment on it, then ask another student or your teacher.

 **Step 4: Write the Final Draft**

a. On your first draft, mark any changes you want to make. You may want to add information or change sentences. Be sure to correct all mistakes.

b. Take another piece of paper, and write your final draft.

c. Edit your paragraph carefully. Then hand it in to your teacher.

Results of the Writing Process

Your teacher will read your paragraph and give you feedback on it. He or she may ask you to rewrite it. Write the new draft, and edit it carefully. Then hand in your old and new drafts together. Staple your new draft on top of the old one.

When you do not need to rewrite a paragraph anymore, put your paper into a folder. Label your folder with your name, your course number, and your teacher's name. Save this folder.

Expansion Activities

Your Journal

Keep making entries in your journal. Write as much as you can. Write as often as you can.

Do not worry about writing perfect sentences. Your journal entries are not formal compositions. A journal entry is like a message to a friend.

Think of your own topics for your journal entries or choose from these topics:

- Write about a favorite food or drink. When and where do you have it? Do you make it, does someone make it for you, or do you buy it?
- Do you have a best friend? Write about a friend who is important to you. What do you like to do together?
- How is the weather today? Do you like this kind of weather? Name a place with great weather. Name a place with terrible weather.
- Draw a picture or put a photo in your journal. Then write about it.
- Where and how do you learn new words in English? Do you write new words in a notebook? What kind of dictionary do you have?

Challenge: *Sleep Habits*

When you write a Challenge paragraph, be sure to follow the steps of the writing process described on pages 45–46.

Write a paragraph about your sleep habits. Here are some questions to help you get started:

- Do you get enough sleep, or are you often tired?
- How many hours of sleep do you need?
- What time do you usually go to bed?
- What time do you usually get up?
- Are weekday and weekend nights the same or different for you?

You can use *My Sleep Habits* as a title. If you wish, begin your paragraph with one of these sentences:

I am happy with my sleep habits.

My sleep habits are not good.

Write your first draft. Ask a friend or a classmate to review your paragraph. You can use the Reviewer's Checklist on page 49 to help you edit. Then prepare a final draft, and give it to your teacher.

Every Picture Tells a Story

Who are they?

Chapter Preview

Chapter Preview

Work with a partner or in a small group. Look at the photo. Then read the two model paragraphs. The writers of these paragraphs have different ideas about the man in the photo. Their paragraphs tell different stories about him. Answer the questions that follow the models.

MODEL

Paragraph 1

The Man in the Photo

The man in the photo is a hardworking man. His name is Ben Smith. He lives in Houston, Texas. He is married. He and his wife have a baby girl. Ben helps take care of the baby. He also works at a post office. He works five nights a week. He is a college student, too. He goes to school part-time. He wants to be a lawyer. Ben Smith leads a busy life.

MODEL

Paragraph 2

A Lucky Man

The man in the photo has an exciting life. His name is Philippe Demay. He is in the music business. He makes music videos in London, England. He has a beautiful wife. She is a model. They go out every night. They go to parties and famous clubs. Philippe has a nice car. It is a Jaguar. I think Philippe is lucky.

Questions about model paragraph 1:

1. What is the topic of the paragraph? _____

2. Read the first sentence again. What is the writer's main idea about the topic? _____

3. What information shows us that Ben is hardworking?

_____

_____

4. Write the **simple present** verbs that complete these sentences from the paragraph.

a. He _____ in Houston, Texas.

b. He _____ married.

c. He and his wife _____ a baby girl.

d. He also _____ at a post office.

e. He _____ to school part-time.

f. He _____ to be a lawyer.

5. Which of the sentences in 4a–f has the verb *be*? Sentence 4 _____

6. What is the last letter of the verb in sentences a, d, e, and f? _____

7. Look at the verb in sentence c. Why is the verb ending different?

_____

Questions about model paragraph 2:

1. What is the topic of the paragraph? _____

2. Read the first sentence again. What is the writer's main idea about the topic? _____

3. What information shows us that Philippe has an exciting life?

_____

_____

4. Write the **adjectives** the writer uses.

a. He has a _____ wife.

b. They go to parties and _____ clubs.

c. Philippe has a _____ car.

d. I think Philippe is _____.

You will write a paragraph about someone in a photo later in this chapter (page 70).

PART 1 | Organization

Topic Sentences

A **topic sentence** comes at the beginning of a paragraph. The topic sentence gives the writer's main idea. A good topic sentence helps readers understand the paragraph.

A topic sentence has two parts: (1) a **topic** — what the paragraph is about, and (2) a **controlling idea** — what the writer is going to focus on in the paragraph. For example, look at this topic sentence:

TOPIC   CONTROLLING IDEA
David Ferreira is a good father.

This topic sentence tells us that the paragraph will be about David Ferreira. The writer will tell us about David as a father. The paragraph will not have other information about David. For example, it will not have information about his education, his friends, or his future plans. It will tell us only about David as a father.

Either the topic or the controlling idea can come first in a topic sentence. Compare these two topic sentences:

CONTROLLING IDEA   TOPIC
There are several reasons why I like **my room**.

TOPIC   CONTROLLING IDEA
I like **my room** for several reasons.

Sometimes the topic and the controlling idea are in two sentences. Look at the example below. Find the topic and the controlling idea.

People sometimes confuse sea lions and seals. These animals are different in several ways. The sea lion has . . .

A sea lion   **A seal**

In this example, the topic is sea lions and seals. The controlling idea — that they are different in several ways — is in the second sentence.

Not all paragraphs begin with a topic sentence, but topic sentences are an important part of academic writing in English. You will need good topic sentences for paragraphs you write for school. You will also need good supporting and concluding sentences. You will learn about these in Chapters 5, 6, and 8.

PRACTICE 3.1

Examining Topic Sentences

Work alone or with a partner. Read each paragraph. Then find the topic sentence. Circle the topic and underline the controlling idea.

1.

A betta makes a good pet. First, it is a beautiful fish, especially in the sunlight. The light brings out its amazing color. Second, it is easy to take care of a betta. Just feed it every day, and give it clean water once a week. Finally, a betta is not expensive. You do not have to spend much money on the fish, its food, or its fishbowl. I tell all my friends to get a betta.

2. It is easy to use an ATM. *ATM* stands for "automated teller machine." Most banks have ATMs now. You can use an ATM to get cash from your bank account. Just put in your ATM card and press the buttons for your PIN (your Personal Identification Number). Then follow the directions on the screen. ATMs are open twenty-four hours a day, seven days a week. They are easy and convenient to use.

3.

The man in the photo has a terrible job. His name is Bob Walker, and he works for Bigg Computers. Every day, customers call him on the phone. They are unhappy about their computers. He does not like to listen to them. Sometimes they get angry, and they yell at Bob. Then he gets angry, too. He needs a new job.

4.

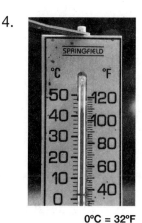

0°C = 32°F

There are two common ways to tell the temperature. One way is to use the Fahrenheit scale. On this scale, water freezes at 32 degrees and boils at 212 degrees. The other way is to use the Celsius (or centigrade) scale. On this scale, water freezes at 0 degrees and boils at 100 degrees. The Celsius system is more common, but in most English-speaking countries, people still use the Fahrenheit system.

PRACTICE 3.2

Choosing the Best Topic Sentence

Work alone or with a partner. Read each paragraph and the three sentences that follow it. Choose the best topic sentence for the paragraph. Write that sentence on the line.

1. _____

_____ For example, butterflies called Painted Ladies fly all the way from Europe to Africa. They also fly from Australia to New Zealand. Monarch butterflies fly from Canada to Mexico. That trip can be 3,000 miles long. It is amazing how far some butterflies can fly.

A monarch butterfly

   a. Butterflies are beautiful.
   b. Some butterflies are great travelers.
   c. Butterflies live in many parts of the world.

2. _____ He played two sports in high school. He was the captain of the wrestling and tennis teams. He is also a good swimmer and a fast runner. He runs every day to stay in shape. Sometimes Kai and I play Ping-Pong together. Kai usually wins. He is good at Ping-Pong, too.

   a. Kai is my friend.
   b. I have a friend at school.
   c. My friend Kai is good at sports.

3. _____

_____ The
letters *a, e, i, o*, and *u* are vowels. The other twenty-one letters are
consonants. The letter *y* can be a consonant or a vowel. For example,
y has a consonant sound in the words *yes* and *you*, but it has a vowel
sound in the words *key* and *play*. Students of English need to learn all
the letters and their sounds.

   a. There are five vowels in English.
   b. English is not an easy language to learn.
   c. The English alphabet has two kinds of letters.

4. _____

_____ The best
beans come from criollo trees. These
trees grow only in Central and South
America. Most beans come from forastero
trees. These trees grow in West Africa.
Finally, the third kind of bean comes from
trinitario trees. These trees grow in both
Africa and the Americas. All three kinds
of cocoa beans are used to make
chocolate.

Cocoa beans in a pod

   a. Some beans grow on trees.
   b. Chocolate is popular around the world.
   c. Chocolate is made from three kinds of cocoa beans.

PRACTICE 3.3

*Supporting a
Topic Sentence*

Work with a partner. Read each topic sentence. Circle the topic and
underline the controlling idea. Then write two examples of sentences
you might find in the paragraph.

1. Cities are exciting places to live.

There are interesting things to do at night, like going to restaurants,

movies, and clubs.

You can meet many new people in cities.

2. Cities have many problems.

Taxes Sor homms are expensive

3. My brother Zamir is good at many things.

  * zamir is good in soccer
  * zamir is good at driving

4. My brother Zamir has some bad habits.

  * he does not listen
  * he does not speak alot

5. It is not easy to learn a new language.

  * It is very hard to learn a new language
  *

6. There are many reasons to learn a new language.

  * Because you can talk to more people
  * Because you are more smart if you know more languages.

PART 2 | Sentence Structure

Subjects of Sentences

In Chapter 1, you learned that every sentence has a subject and a verb. Here is more information about subjects.

Rules	Examples
1. A subject can be a noun or a subject pronoun.	**Alex** has a car. **He** likes to drive.
2. The subject comes before the verb in a statement.	On weekdays, **he** <u>takes</u> the bus to work.
3. A verb can have more than one subject.	**Alex** and **his friends** <u>have</u> cars.

PRACTICE 3.4

Identifying Subjects and Verbs

Work alone or with a partner. Find the subject and the verb in each sentence. Circle the subject and write *S* above it. Underline the verb and write *V* above it.

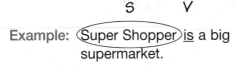

                S   V

Example: (Super Shopper) is a big supermarket.

1. We buy most of our food at Super Shopper.

2. It sells local food and food from around the world.

3. I get fruit and vegetables in the produce department.

4. The fruit is fresh and colorful.

5. The bread in the bakery smells wonderful.

6. My wife and I go to Super Shopper on Fridays.

7. On weekends, the store is full of shoppers.

8. The lines sometimes get very long.

What Makes a Complete Sentence?

Look at these groups of words. They are not complete sentences.

Is friendly.

Has five people in her family.

Something is missing. Who is friendly? Who has five people in her family? The subjects are missing. A sentence must have a subject. For example, you could write:

Bella is friendly.

She has five people in her family.

Look at these groups of words. They are not complete sentences either. Something is missing.

My brother in Los Angeles.

Apples, bananas, and pears good.

What is missing? There are no verbs. There must be a verb in a sentence. For example, you could write:

My brother **is** in Los Angeles.

Apples, bananas, and pears **taste** good.

PRACTICE 3.5

Editing: Recognizing Complete Sentences

Work alone or with a partner. Look at each sentence. Check (✓) **Complete** or **Incomplete**. For each incomplete sentence, tell what is missing. Write *No subject* or *No verb*. Then correct the incomplete sentences.

	Complete	Incomplete	What's the problem?
1. a. The capital of China is Beijing.	✓		
b. Beijing *is* a big city.		✓	No verb
c. The city 5,000 years old.		✓	
2. a. San Francisco has many attractions.	✓		
b. Is cool in the summer.		✓	
3. a. Many tourists travel to Mexico.			✓
b. Visit the beaches there.	✓	✓	
4. a. The beaches of Thailand nice, too.		✓	✓
b. Tourists like the beaches of Thailand.	✓		
c. Many tourists postcards.		✓	
5. a. Sydney a city in Australia.		✓	✓
b. It has a famous opera house.			
c. Many visitors to Sydney.		✓	

PRACTICE 3.6

*Editing:
Incomplete
Sentences*

Work alone or with a partner. Find the seven incomplete sentences in this paragraph. Make corrections. The first incomplete sentence has been corrected for you.

> I want to tell you about my friend Yasmin. She lives in Seattle,
> She is
> Washington. ~~Is~~ young and single. She twenty-four years old. Works in
> a women's clothing store. Is a nice place to buy clothes. Yasmin likes
> her job. Clothes very important to her. Loves to shop. She spends her
> money on new clothes and shoes. She has a plan to open a clothing
> store. Wants to have her own business. It is a good idea.

PRACTICE 3.7

*Editing:
Incomplete
Sentences*

Work alone or with a partner. Find the incomplete sentences. Make corrections.

> The name of my hometown is I-Lan. My parents and my
> grandparents there. Is a small city in the countryside of Taiwan.
> Has a population of 30,000. The weather in I-Lan changes with the
> seasons. The winter wet and cool. The summer hot and humid.
> We have typhoons from August through October. I-Lan has good
> weather for plants. Is famous for growing vegetables. It a nice
> place to live.

PART 3 | Grammar and Vocabulary

Adjectives

The different types of words are called the **parts of speech**. Verbs and nouns are two of the parts of speech. **Adjectives** are another part of speech. An adjective describes a noun or a subject pronoun.

The **boldfaced** words in the three sentences below are adjectives. The words they describe are underlined.

The <u>elevator</u> is **full**.　　　<u>He</u> is **tall**.　　　I like my **new** <u>phone</u>.

You can use adjectives in several ways.

Rules	Examples			
			Be + Adjective	
1. Use *be* + an adjective.	Paris I They		<u>is</u> **beautiful**. <u>am</u> not **Chinese**. <u>are</u> **tall** and **handsome**.	
			Adjective + Noun	
2. Use an adjective + a noun.	You are Ali has		a **good** <u>friend</u>. **short, dark** <u>hair</u>. **Fresh** <u>blueberries</u>	taste good.
3. Do not add -*s* to adjectives.	This building is **old**. These buildings are **olds**.			

See Appendix J for information about the order of adjectives before a noun.

PRACTICE 3.8

*Adjectives
and the Words
They Describe*

Work alone or with a partner. The **boldfaced** words in this paragraph are adjectives. Underline the words (nouns or subject pronouns) that the adjectives describe.

I have a **favorite** <u>beach</u>. It has **soft**, **white** sand and **nice**, **clean** water. In the summer, the beach is **hot**. I sit under a **big** umbrella, and I often go into the **cool** water. This beach is a **good** place to swim. The waves are usually **small**. Sometimes I spend the **whole** day at the beach. On **other** days, I go to the beach in the **late** afternoon or in the **early** evening. It is **quiet** at that time.

Waves

PRACTICE 3.9

*Identifying
Adjectives*

Work alone or with a partner. Circle the twelve adjectives in this paragraph. The first adjective is circled for you.

Carlos likes living in Westfield, Massachusetts. It is a (small) and quiet town. The streets are narrow. Along the streets there are many big trees. They are beautiful. Westfield has great parks, too. Stanley Park is Carlos's favorite park. It is large and green. There are nice fields for playing baseball and new courts for playing basketball. Carlos has a good time in the park with his friends.

PRACTICE 3.10

*Understanding
Common
Adjectives*

A. Look at the adjectives in this list. Mark each word *0, 1,* or *2.*

0 = I know nothing about this word.

1 = I know a little about this word.

2 = I use this word in writing and speaking.

busy ____	free ____	nervous ____
careful ____	funny ____	single ____
difficult ____	interesting ____	tired ____
exciting ____	married ____	unusual ____
expensive ____	neat ____	wonderful ____

B. Choose three words that you marked *0* or *1*. Ask an English speaker about their meanings, or look them up in the dictionary. Use each of the three words in a sentence.

_____

_____

_____

PRACTICE 3.11

Using Adjectives

Take a piece of paper. Write sentences with adjectives. Follow the directions.

Examples: Name a food and describe it. Candy is sweet.

Name a song and describe it. "Happy Birthday" is a famous song.

1. Name a movie and describe it.
2. Name a friend and describe him or her.
3. Name a city and describe it.
4. Name an actor and describe him or her.
5. Name a kind of car and describe it.
6. Name a kind of animal and describe it.
7. Describe your hair.
8. Describe your eyes.

The Simple Present

The **simple present** tense has two main uses. Use simple present verbs to:

(1) state facts — things that are true.

The sun **rises** in the east.

People **need** food and water.

(2) describe routines and habits — actions that happen again and again.

I always **eat** lunch with my friends.

The store **opens** at 9:00 A.M. every day.

Simple Present Tense: Affirmative Statements

Singular Subject	Verb
I	**sleep**.
You	
He	**sleeps**.
She	
It	
The cat	

Plural Subject	Verb
We	**sleep**.
You	
They	
The cats	

The form of a simple present verb depends on the subject.

Rules	Examples
1. Use the base form of the verb after *I, you, we, they,* and plural noun subjects.	We **talk** a lot. Some people **worry** too much.
2. Verbs after *he, she, it,* or singular noun subjects end in *-s, -es,* or *-ies.* These are **third person singular** subjects and verbs.	He **talks** a lot. My mother **worries** too much.
3. The verb *have* is **irregular**. It is not like other verbs.	I/You/We/They **have** brown eyes. He/She/It **has** blue eyes.

See Appendix E for spelling rules for third person singular verbs.

PRACTICE 3.12

Simple Present Verbs in Affirmative Statements

Circle the correct form of the verb.

1. I (keep)/ keeps) photos in my wallet.

2. I (carry / carries) photos of my family.

3. We sometimes (look / looks) at photos in class.

4. The teacher (have / has) many photos of people and places.

5. She (use / uses) a digital camera.

6. It (take / takes) good photos.

7. This photo (show / shows) my children.

8. You (have / has) a beautiful family.

PRACTICE 3.13

Spelling Third Person Singular Verbs

Write the third person singular form of each verb. See Appendix E for help.

1. fly	_____flies_____	8. catch	_____
2. wash	_____	9. do	_____
3. cook	_____	10. give	_____
4. fix	_____	11. hurry	_____
5. study	_____	12. have	_____
6. go	_____	13. rain	_____
7. brush	_____	14. snow	_____

PRACTICE 3.14

Verbs with Third Person Subjects: Singular and Plural

Complete the sentences. Use the verbs in parentheses.

1. (treat) Doctors ____treat____ patients.

2. (build) Carpenters _____ furniture and houses.

3. (write) A programmer _____ computer software.

4. (prepare) A cook _____ meals.

5. (clean) Window washers _____ windows.

6. (deliver) A mail carrier _____ letters and packages.

7. (help) A salesclerk _____ customers in a store.

8. (serve) A waiter _____ customers in a restaurant.

9. (fly) Pilots _____ airplanes.

10. (do) Students _____ homework.

Simple Present: Negative Statements

Singular Subject	Do/Does	Not	Base Verb
I	do		
You			
He	does	not	run.
She			
It			
The cat			

Plural Subject	Do	Not	Base Verb
We			
You			
They	do	not	run.
The cats			

See Appendix E for contractions.

PRACTICE 3.15

Simple Present Verbs in Negative Statements

Underline the verb in the first statement. Use the same verb in the second statement, but make it negative.

1. Baseball players <u>catch</u> baseballs. Soccer players __do not catch__ soccer balls.

2. Soccer players kick soccer balls. Tennis players _____ tennis balls.

3. A baseball player needs a glove. A soccer player _____ a glove.

4. Football players wear cleats. Tennis players _____ cleats.

5. A tennis player uses a racket. A football player _____ a racket.

6. Soccer players score goals. Baseball players _____ goals.

7. A football player has a helmet. A soccer player _____ a helmet.

8. I like soccer and baseball. I _____ tennis or football.

PRACTICE 3.16

Affirmative and Negative Statements

A. Complete the paragraph. Write the correct forms of the verbs in parentheses.

I really ___*like*___ winter. My city, Montreal, Québec, _____

(1. like)   (2. get)

a lot of snow. I _____ snowy weather. My friends and

(3. like)

I _____ playing in the snow. Winter _____ a long time in

(4. enjoy)   (5. last)

Montreal. We _____ warm clothes here. The weather _____

(6. need)   (7. get)

very cold. I _____ hot cocoa to warm up. We _____ fires

(8. drink)   (9. build)

in the fireplace. Winter _____ my favorite season.

(10. be)

B. Rewrite the paragraph. Change *Montreal, Québec* to *New Orleans, Louisiana*. Make all the verbs negative.

<u>   I really do not like winter. My city, New Orleans, Louisiana, does not get</u>

<u>a lot of snow.   </u>

_____

_____

_____

_____

_____

PRACTICE 3.17

Editing: Errors in Simple Present Verbs

Work alone or with a partner. Find the verb error in each statement. Make corrections.

Examples: My friend ~~speak~~ *speaks* Arabic. He ~~is~~ *does* not speak English.

1. The movie start at 9:30 P.M.

2. Children likes candy.

3. Mr. Abo is goes to work by car.

4. Pilar watchs TV in the evening.

5. It does not cold today.

6. That store sell shoes.

7. People needs sleep.

8. He does not has a car.

9. They do not married.

10. My friends speak Spanish, but they are not speak French.

PART 4 | The Writing Process

Your Paragraph: *The Face in the Photo*

You are going to write a paragraph about a person in a photograph, like the model paragraphs on page 53. You will need to use your **imagination**.

imagination = the ability to form new ideas or pictures in your mind

A writer with a great imagination

 **Step 1: Prewrite**

a. Look at the people in the four photos on page 71. Choose one person to write about. Imagine that you know the person well.

A.

B.

C.

D.

b. On a piece of paper, make a list of ideas about the person in your photo. Do not write complete sentences. Just make notes.

c. Find a partner who has chosen a different photo. Ask your partner about the person in his or her photo. For example, ask:

What is his/her name?

Where is he/she from?

Where does he/she live?

How old is he/she?

Does he/she have a family?

Does he/she go to school?

Does he/she have a job?

What does he/she like to do for fun?

What do you think about his/her life?

d. Add to your notes or make any changes you want.

   **Step 2: Write**

a. Choose a title for your paragraph. You can use *The Man/Woman in the Photo* if you like.

b. Begin your paragraph with a topic sentence. Identify the person (which photo are you writing about?), and state your main idea about him or her. This will be the controlling idea about your topic. For example, you can use one of these statements:

The woman in photo A has a _____ life.

The man in photo B is a _____ person.

Add an adjective to describe the person or the person's life. In your paragraph, you must show your readers why that adjective is true.

c. Use your notes to complete your first draft.

   **Step 3: Edit**

a. Read your paragraph again. It may help you to read it out loud. Make changes if needed.

b. Edit your paragraph carefully. Check for mistakes before you show it to anyone.

c. Peer review: Exchange papers with a partner. Follow the Reviewer's Checklist on page 73. Check (✓) each box when you finish that step.

Reviewer's Checklist — Chapter 3

Your partner's name: _____

<u>Content</u>

☐ Read all of your partner's paragraph.

☐ Underline any part of the paragraph you do not understand. Ask your partner to explain it.

☐ Circle the topic sentence. Write *TS* on the paper if there is no topic sentence.

☐ Ask questions if you want more information about the person in the photo.

<u>Form</u>

Look at these parts of your partner's paper. Mark any problems on the paper in pencil. Put a question mark (?) if you are not sure about something. (See Henry Liu's first draft on page 46 for an example of how to mark a paper.)

☐ the heading   ☐ capital letters and periods

☐ the title   ☐ a subject in every sentence

☐ indenting the first sentence   ☐ a verb for every subject

d. Return your partner's paper. Say something nice about it, such as "It's a good first draft" or "I like your ideas."

e. Look at your own paper. If you do not agree with a comment on it, then ask another student or your teacher.

Step 4: Write the Final Draft

a. On your first draft, mark any changes you want to make. Then take another piece of paper and write a new draft.

b. Edit your paragraph carefully. Then hand it in to your teacher.

Results of the Writing Process

Your teacher will read your paragraph and give you feedback on it. He or she may ask you to rewrite it. Then you will write a new draft. Hand in your old and new drafts together. Staple your new draft on top of the old one.

When you do not need to write another draft, put your paper in your folder.

Expansion Activities

Your Journal

Continue making entries in your journal. Remember to read your teacher's comments. Sometimes your teacher will write questions in your journal. Write the answers, or talk to your teacher about the questions.

If you need a topic for a journal entry, maybe these ideas will help:

- Who do you talk to on the phone? Name three people. When do you talk to them? What kinds of things do you usually talk about?
- Name a place that you think is beautiful. What makes it beautiful?
- Do you have a pet? Write about your pet, or write about an animal that interests you.
- Do you like to watch movies? What kinds of movies do you like most? Name a movie that you have seen recently. Do you think your teacher would like it?
- When do you usually do your homework? Where do you do it? Do you work alone, or do you work with other people? Do you listen to music while you work? Do you eat or drink while you work?

Challenge: *An Important Person*

Write a paragraph about a person who is important to you. You can use the person's name as a title, or use the title *Someone I Care About* if you like.

Start by writing some notes about this person. The list of questions on page 71 might help you get ideas. Then write a first draft. Remember to begin your paragraph with a topic sentence. For example, you could write *My friend Elizabeth is very important in my life.*

Ask a friend or a classmate to review your first draft. Use the Reviewer's Checklist on page 73. Prepare a final draft, and give it to your teacher.

4 Saturdays

Saturday in the park

Chapter Preview

Chapter Preview

Work with a partner or in a small group. Read the two model paragraphs. Answer the questions that follow.

MODEL

Paragraph 1

Karl's Saturdays

Saturday is a busy day for Karl. He gets up early. Then he works from 6:00 A.M. to 2:00 P.M. After work, he goes home. He plays with his little boy in the afternoon. He helps his wife. They do chores. Sometimes they go shopping or run errands. They usually have dinner at home. In the evening, Karl puts his son to bed. Then he finally has free time. He and his wife often watch a movie.

MODEL

Paragraph 2

Tomiko's Favorite Day

Saturday is Tomiko's favorite day. She always sleeps late in the morning. She sometimes gets up at noon. Then she usually meets her friends in the dining hall. In the afternoon, they spend time outside or go shopping. It depends on the weather. On Saturday evenings, she likes to dress up and go out. She and her friends often go to the movies or to a party. Tomiko loves Saturdays.

Questions about model paragraph 1:

1. What is the topic sentence? Copy it on the line below. Circle the topic and underline the controlling idea.

_____

2. What information does the writer give about Karl's Saturdays? Check (✓) your answers.

☐ what Karl does in the morning

☐ what he does in the afternoon

☐ what he does in the evening

☐ Karl's feelings about Saturdays

3. What word means "small jobs at home"? _____

4. What word means "short trips for shopping or other business"?
_____

5. Write the simple present verbs that the writer uses.

  a. They _____ chores.

  b. Sometimes they _____ shopping or
  _____ errands.

  c. They usually _____ dinner at home.

  d. In the evening, Karl _____ his son to bed.

  e. Then he finally _____ free time.

Questions about model paragraph 2:

1. What is the topic sentence? Copy it on the line below. Circle the topic and underline the controlling idea.

_____

2. What information does the writer give about Tomiko's Saturdays?

  ☐ what Tomiko does in the morning

  ☐ what she does in the afternoon

  ☐ what she does in the evening

  ☐ Tomiko's feelings about Saturdays

3. Talk about what you think this sentence means in the paragraph: *It depends on the weather.*

4. What two-word phrase means "put on nice clothes"?

_____

5. Write the **adverbs of frequency** that the writer uses.

a. She _____ sleeps late in the morning.

b. She _____ gets up at noon.

c. Then she _____ meets her friends in the dining hall.

d. She and her friends _____ go to the movies or to a party.

You will interview a classmate and write a paragraph about his or her Saturday activities later in this chapter (page 92).

PART 1 | Organization

Time Order

When you write, you must think about **organization** — planning and presenting information in a clear order. Writers need to organize information to make it easy for people to read. There are many ways to do this.

One way to organize information is to put it in **time order** (also called *chronological order*). This means writing about events in the order in which they happen. Start with the first or earliest event, and then tell what happens after that.

Time-order words also help make information clear to the reader. Here are some examples of time-order words:

First,   Next,   Then   After that,   Later,   Finally,

These words go at the beginning of sentences. A comma follows each one except *Then*. Do not put a comma after *Then*.

Learn about prepositional phrases to describe time on page 88.

PRACTICE 4.1

Time-Order Words

Underline the six time-order words in this paragraph. The first one is underlined for you.

Luis and Ada have a daily routine at their bookstore. They always get to the store at 8:30 A.M. <u>First</u>, Luis unlocks the door and turns on the lights. Next, he turns on the coffeemaker, and Ada starts up the computer. Then they put new books on the shelves and in the store window. After that, they open for business. Luis begins working with customers in the store, and Ada works on the computer. Later, they change places. They clean the store together at the end of the day. Finally, they close up and go home.

PRACTICE 4.2

Time-Order Words

Work alone or with a partner. Add the words in the box to the paragraph below. There is more than one correct answer in some cases.

After	Finally	~~First~~	Later	Next	Then

Sunday is a relaxing day for George. He gets up at 9:30 or 10:00 in the morning. (1) __First__, he takes a shower. (2) _____, he has breakfast. (3) _____ he reads the newspaper. (4) _____ that, he washes his car. In the afternoon, he watches his favorite TV show, *Sports World*. (5) _____, he orders pizza for supper. In the evening, he calls his mother and his brothers. (6) _____, he gets into bed and reads.

PRACTICE 4.3

Time Order

Number the sentences in order by time. Then write them as a paragraph on the lines.

____ First, she changes her clothes.

__1__ Eva likes to spend quiet evenings at home.

____ She eats her dinner and reads the newspaper.

_____ She usually gets home from work at 5:45 P.M.

_____ Finally, she sits down to watch TV.

_____ After dinner, she does the dishes.

_____ Then she goes to the kitchen and makes dinner.

Eva likes to spend quiet evenings at home.
_____

_____

_____

_____

_____

_____

_____

PART 2 | Sentence Structure and Vocabulary

Simple Sentence Patterns I

There are several kinds of sentences in English. First, there are **simple sentences**. A simple sentence has one subject-verb combination. Look at these two patterns for simple sentences:

1 **subject** + 1 **verb**	I **like** blue.
1 **subject** + 1 **verb**	Blue **is** a nice color.
2 **subjects** + 1 **verb**	Alfredo and I **like** red.
2 **subjects** + 1 **verb**	Red and blue **are** nice colors.

The two subjects go with the same verb, so there is one subject-verb combination.

Use *(Someone) and I* as a subject. Do not use *Me and (someone)* as a subject.

My friends and I play tennis.

NOT: ~~Me and my friends~~ play tennis.

PRACTICE 4.4

Simple Sentence Patterns

Underline the verbs and write *V* above them. Circle the subjects and write *S* above them.

       S   S V

1. (Red and blue) <u>are</u> my favorite colors.

2. The sky and the ocean are blue.

3. The color blue seems peaceful.

4. Both men and women usually like blue.

5. Red is a strong and exciting color.

6. In China, red means "happiness."

7. Red and blue are two of the primary colors.

8. The other primary color is yellow.

9. The secondary colors are orange, green, and purple.

10. Rainbows have all the primary and secondary colors.

Adverbs of Frequency

The Meanings of Adverbs of Frequency

Adverbs of frequency tell how often something happens.

How often do they eat breakfast?	Su	M	Tu	W	Th	F	Sa	
Al **always** eats breakfast.	✓	✓	✓	✓	✓	✓	✓	100%
Uma **usually** eats breakfast.		✓	✓	✓	✓	✓	✓	
Oliva **often** eats breakfast.		✓		✓		✓	✓	
Saeed **sometimes** eats breakfast.	✓			✓				
Norberto **never** eats breakfast.								0%

Position of Adverbs of Frequency in Affirmative Statements

Rules	Examples			
1. In most affirmative statements: Put the adverb after the subject and before the verb.	**Subject**	**Adverb**	**Verb**	
	I Maggie	**usually** **never**	arrive comes	at 8:55 A.M. on time.
2. In statements with *be*: Put the adverb after *be*.	**Subject**	*Be*	**Adverb**	
	I George	am is	**often** **usually**	early. late.

Sometimes can also come at the beginning or at the end of an affirmative statement.

Sometimes we order pizza.
We **sometimes** order pizza.
We order pizza **sometimes**.

PRACTICE 4.5
Adverbs of Frequency

Add the adverb of frequency in parentheses to the affirmative statement.

Happy Mother's Day!

1. (often) Schools ^often^ close on holidays.

2. (never) Some people celebrate the new year on January 1.

3. (usually) Mother's Day is a popular holiday.

4. (always) The dates of some holidays change, depending on the moon.

5. (usually) People think of Valentine's Day as a day for people in love.

6. (always) Valentine's Day is on February 14.

7. (often) Workers have a holiday in their honor.

8. (never) Some women work on International Women's Day.

PRACTICE 4.6
Sometimes in Affirmative Statements

Rewrite each statement three times. Add *sometimes* in three different positions.

1. My family has a special holiday meal.

_____

_____

_____

2. Stores are closed on holidays.

_____

_____

_____

Position of Adverbs of Frequency in Negative Statements

Rules	Examples			
		Not	**Adverb**	
...ly, and *often* after *not*.	He does They are	not not	**always** **often**	sleep well. late.
...the beginning of the	**Sometimes** he does not understand the homework.			
...th *never*.	is never He ~~isn't never~~ on time.			

...write each negative statement. Add the adverb in parentheses. ...member: Do not use *not* and *never* together.

Example: I am not at home on New Year's Eve. (never)

I am never at home on New Year's Eve.

1. People in different countries do not have the same holidays. (always)

_____

2. Halloween is not an important holiday outside the United States. (usually)

_____

3. Father's Day is not on a weekday in the United States. (never)

_____

4. Some businesses do not close on holidays. (never)

_____

5. For example, airports do not close on holidays. (often)

_____

6. People do not celebrate every holiday in the same way. (usually)

_____

7. In some countries, birthdays are not special days. (usually)

_____

8. I do not forget my birthday. (never)

_____

PRACTICE 4.8

Using Adverbs of Frequency

Take a piece of paper. Write complete sentences to answer the questions. Use at least three different adverbs of frequency.

Examples: Do you ever watch the news?
I do not usually watch the news.

Are you ever tired in class?
I am often tired in class on Mondays.

1. Do you drink milk?
2. Are you ever late for class?
3. Do you ever write letters?
4. Are you in bed at 11:00 P.M.?
5. Do you surf the Internet?
6. Are you ever in a bad mood?
7. Do you go shopping on weekends?
8. Do you ever get hungry in class?

PART 3 | Grammar and Mechanics

Common Verbs

Some verbs are very common. English speakers use them every day. These verbs have many meanings.

Pay attention to the words after the four common verbs in this chart. If you can, add other examples of words that can follow each verb.

Base Form	Simple Present Forms	Common Ways to Use the Verb
1. have	have, has	have (a possession), have (a family member), have money have fun, have a party, have a baby, have breakfast Other examples: ___have time___ _____
2. do	do, does	do homework do the dishes, do laundry, do chores Other examples: _____ _____
3. make	make, makes	make coffee, make a sandwich, make dinner make a phone call make a mistake, make an appointment Other examples: _____ _____
4. get	get, gets	get sick, get hungry, get tired, get married get (something) at the store get to (a place) Other examples: _____ _____

When you see these common verbs, pay attention to the words that follow them.

The verb *be* is also very common. See page 40 for information about how *be* combines with other words.

PRACTICE 4.9

Word Partners

A. Read the paragraph. Circle the forms of *have, do, make,* and *get.* Underline the words that follow these verbs.

Every morning, Ebru (does) the same thing. At 8:00 A.M., she gets the bus at the end of her street. She gets to school at about 8:30 A.M. She has time before her first class, so she goes to the cafeteria and has coffee. There are usually many other students there. Some students are having breakfast, some are doing homework, and some are making phone calls. Sometimes she sees a classmate in the cafeteria, and they talk. Ebru is making new friends at school. At 8:55 A.M., she leaves the cafeteria, and she gets to her classroom by 9:00 A.M.

B. Look at the words you underlined. Some are already in the chart on page 87. Add new examples to the chart under "Other examples."

PRACTICE 4.10

Using Common Verbs

Take a piece of paper. Write three true statements using each verb.

Example: have   I have a new watch.
                   I have tea in the morning.
                   I have a son named Ken.

1. have   3. make
2. do   4. get

Using Prepositions to Show Time

Prepositions are usually small words, such as *in, at, by,* and *with.* A preposition and a noun form a **prepositional phrase**. Prepositional phrases have many uses. For example, they can be **time expressions**. Time expressions tell when something happens.

PREP. + NOUN
On Saturdays, I like to sleep late.

PREP. + NOUN
I sometimes get up **in the afternoon**.

A time expression can go at the beginning or at the end of a sentence. Put a comma after a time expression at the beginning of a sentence.

There are many rules for using prepositions to show time. Here are four rules you need to know.

Rules	Examples
1. Use *on* + a day or days.	Do we have class **on Friday**? They see each other **on weekends**.
2. Use *in* + a part of the day. Exception: Use *at* + *night*.	Call me **in the morning**. He gets home late **at night**.
3. Use *at* + a time.	He starts work **at 8:30 A.M.** Lunch is **at noon**.
4. Use *from* + a starting point + *to* + the end point.	**From 7:00 to 10:00 P.M.**, he studies. The course runs **from January to May**.

See pages 128–130, and 169 for more information on prepositions.

PRACTICE 4.11

Prepositions in Time Expressions

Underline the seven time expressions with prepositions. The first one is underlined for you.

The Rock and Roll Hall of Fame in Cleveland, Ohio, is a big attraction. Half a million people visit each year. The hall is usually open from 10:00 A.M. to 5:30 P.M. On Wednesdays, it is also open in the evening. In the summer (from Memorial Day to Labor Day), it stays open late on Saturdays, too. The hall is closed only on Thanksgiving and Christmas. There are exhibits, films, concerts, and a museum store. It is a great place for rock and roll fans to visit.

PRACTICE 4.12

Prepositions in Time Expressions

Complete the sentences. Use *in, on, at, from*, or *to* to show time.

1. Do you dream _____ night?

2. The movie runs _____ 7:00 P.M. _____ 8:50 P.M.

3. We have class _____ Tuesdays and Thursdays.

4. What do you do _____ the evening?

5. The train leaves _____ 4:35 P.M.

6. I usually have a snack _____ the afternoon.

7. The office is open only _____ weekdays.

8. The school year goes _____ September _____ June.

Titles

A **title** is the name of a book, a song, a story, or a movie. Titles are not usually sentences. They are usually just a few words. A title can be one word, such as *Titanic* or *Superman*.

When you write a paragraph for an assignment in this book, it should have a title. A title gives the reader a little information about your paragraph, but the real introduction to your paragraph comes in your topic sentence. Sometimes your topic sentence must repeat words from the title. Look at these examples:

Do this:

My Friend Ray
I have a good friend named Ray. He is always . . .

Do not do this:

My Friend Ray
He is a good friend. He is always . . .

Writer's Tip

It is a good idea to write your paragraph before you write your title. Finish your first draft, check your topic sentence, and then add a title.

Capitalization in Titles *are not sientences*

Rules	Examples
1. Capitalize the first letter of the first word of a title.	**M**y Life **T**he Phantom of the Opera
2. Capitalize every noun, verb, pronoun, adjective, and adverb in a title. Do not capitalize *a, an, the,* or prepositions.	**A D**ay at the **R**aces **J**ourney to the **C**enter of the **E**arth **T**ake **M**e **O**ut to the **B**all **G**ame
3. Do not put a period after your title.	Getting Ready for the Day
4. Do not put quotation marks (" ") around your title.	Jae Yoon's Favorite Day

---

PRACTICE 4.13

Capital Letters in Titles

Work alone or with a partner. Rewrite each title with the capital letters needed.

1. fundamentals of academic writing

   <u>Fundamentals of Academic Writing</u>

2. first steps in academic writing

   F   S   A   W

3. the adventures of Tom Sawyer

   T A

4. gone with the wind

   G

5. a wrinkle in time

   A W T

6. the lord of the rings

   T L R

7. introduction to psychology

   I P

8. around the world in eighty days

   A

PRACTICE 4.14

Inventing Titles

Work with a partner. Think of good titles for books or movies about the topics below.

Example: two young people in love
First and Last Love

1. a group of teenagers in a scary place

   _____

2. a big storm, like a hurricane or typhoon

   _____

3. a trip on a spaceship in the future

   _____

4. two people getting married at age eighty

   _____

5. a bank robbery

   _____

6. two boys away from home

   _____

PART 4 | The Writing Process

Your Paragraph: *My Partner's Saturdays*

You are going to interview a classmate about what he or she usually does on Saturdays. Then you are going to use the information to write a paragraph like the models on page 77.

Step 1: Prewrite

a. Work with a partner. Ask your partner, "What do you usually do on Saturdays?" Listen and take notes in the chart on page 93. Do not write complete sentences.

in the morning	
in the afternoon	
in the evening	

b. What adjective best describes your partner's Saturdays? Talk with your partner about this question. There are examples of adjectives in the box below. If you wish, you can use one of these adjectives in your topic sentence.

| boring | busy | difficult | exciting | interesting | relaxing |

c. Write a topic sentence for your paragraph. Look at the models on page 77 for ideas.

 **Step 2: Write**

a. Begin your paragraph with your topic sentence.

b. Continue writing your first draft, using your notes from Step 1.

c. Use time-order words, time expressions with prepositions, and adverbs of frequency as needed.

d. Give your paragraph a title.

Step 3: Edit

a. Read your paragraph again. It may help you to read it out loud. Make changes if needed.

b. Edit your paragraph carefully. Check for mistakes before you show it to anyone.

c. Peer review: Exchange papers with the partner that you wrote about. Follow the Reviewer's Checklist below. Check (✓) each box when you finish that step.

Reviewer's Checklist — Chapter 4

Your partner's name: _____

Content

☐ Read all of your partner's paragraph.

☐ Underline any part of the paragraph you do not understand. Ask your partner to explain it.

☐ Tell your partner if any information is not correct.

☐ Circle the topic sentence. Write *TS* on the paper if there is no topic sentence.

Form

Look at these parts of your partner's paper. Mark any problems on the paper in pencil. Put a question mark (?) if you are not sure about something. (See Henry Liu's first draft on page 46 for an example of how to mark a paper.)

☐ the title

☐ a subject in every sentence

☐ a verb for every subject

☐ the use of words to show time (time-order words, time expressions with prepositions, adverbs of frequency)

---

d. Return your partner's paper. Say something nice about it, such as "I liked reading this" or "Good job."

e. Look at your own paper. If you do not agree with a comment on it, then ask another student or your teacher.

Step 4: Write the Final Draft

a. On your first draft, mark any changes you want to make. Then take another piece of paper and write a new draft.

b. Edit your paragraph carefully. Then hand it in to your teacher.

Results of the Writing Process

Your teacher will give you feedback on your paragraph. Look carefully at your teacher's comments and marks on the paper. Ask your teacher about anything you do not understand. Your teacher may ask you to write a new draft.

Check your new draft carefully before you hand it in. Remember to hand in your old and new drafts together, with the new draft on top.

When you do not need to rewrite a paragraph any more, put it in your folder.

Expansion Activities

Your Journal

Continue making entries in your journal. Do not worry about making mistakes. Your journal is a good place to experiment with new words.

If you need a topic for a journal entry, try one of these ideas:

- What is your favorite color? Do you have more than one favorite? What colors do you usually wear?
- Write about a friend who has a job. What does your friend do? Where and when does your friend work? Do you think that he or she has a good job?
- Name an island you want to visit. What do you know about this island? Why do you want to go there?
- What are the seasons of the year where you live? Which season do you like most? Why?
- What languages do you know? Why are you learning English? Tell how you feel about learning English.

Challenge: *My Favorite Holiday*

Write a paragraph about your favorite holiday. Begin by taking notes. What do you usually do on this day? Organize your notes by time. If you want, you can make a chart like the one on page 93.

Use your notes to write a paragraph. Begin your paragraph with a topic sentence, such as *Independence Day is always a lot of fun* or *New Year's Eve is my favorite holiday*. Remember to give your paragraph a title.

Ask a friend or a classmate to review your first draft. Use the Reviewer's Checklist on page 94. Prepare a final draft, and give it to your teacher.

What's Going On?

What's up?

Chapter Preview

Part 1: Organization
Topic Sentences and Supporting Sentences I

Part 2: Sentence Structure
Simple Sentence Patterns II

Part 3: Grammar
The Present Progressive
Non-Action Verbs

Part 4: The Writing Process
Your Paragraph: *What Is Happening in This Photo*?
Results of the Writing Process

Expansion Activities

Chapter Preview

Work with a partner or in a small group. Read the two model paragraphs. Answer the questions that follow.

A.   B.

MODEL

Paragraph 1

> ### Tap Dancers
> Photo A shows a boy and his grandfather. They look happy. The boy is looking up at his grandfather and smiling. His grandfather is teaching him to tap dance. They are dancing on the sidewalk in front of their house. They are doing the same step. The sun is shining, and it looks like summer. It is a beautiful day, and they are having fun.

MODEL

Paragraph 2

> ### At the Hair Salon
> The young woman in photo B looks nervous. She is at a hair salon. A man is cutting her hair. She is sitting, and she has a towel around her shoulders. The man is standing in back of her. He is holding her hair with one hand. He has a pair of scissors in his other hand. He is saying something. She is trying to smile. She is wondering, "What is he doing? Am I making a mistake?"

Questions about model paragraph 1:

1. The writer's topic and controlling idea are in the first two sentences. Copy them on the line below. Circle the topic and underline the controlling idea.

   _____

2. What details does the writer give in describing photo A? Check (✓) your answers.

   ☐ the people   ☐ the weather   ☐ the people's clothes

   ☐ the place   ☐ the people's actions ☐ the people's feelings

3. What do you think is the meaning of *it looks like summer*?

4. Write the **present progressive** verbs to complete these sentences from the paragraph.

   a. The boy _____ up at his grandfather and

      _____ .

   b. They _____ the same step.

   c. The sun _____ , and it looks like summer.

Questions about model paragraph 2:

1. What is the topic sentence? Copy it on the line below. Circle the topic and underline the controlling idea.

   _____

2. The writer thinks the woman is nervous. Do you agree?

   ☐ Yes. She is nervous because _____

   ☐ No. I think the woman looks _____

3. What are the two different meanings of the verb *look* in these two sentences?

   > The young woman looks nervous.

   > He is looking at his grandfather.

4. Find and write the sentences that use these words.

a. He / say / something _____

b. She / try / to smile _____

c. I / make / a mistake _____

You will write a paragraph describing a photo later in this chapter (page 114).

PART 1 | Organization

Topic Sentences and Supporting Sentences I

Support for the Topic Sentence

In Chapter 3, you learned about topic sentences. The sentences that follow a topic sentence are called **supporting sentences**. They support the topic sentence in the same way that the legs of a table support the tabletop. Supporting sentences show the reader why the topic sentence is true.

The supporting sentences show us why Jack is lucky.

Some paragraphs end with a **concluding sentence**. You will learn more about concluding sentences in Chapter 8.

Look at the three parts of this paragraph:

3-7

TOPIC SENTENCE

SUPPORTING SENTENCES

(THE BODY OF THE PARAGRAPH)

CONCLUDING SENTENCE

The human heart is a hard worker. It does not stop to take breaks. It works all day and all night, day after day. The heart pumps blood into the lungs. There, the blood picks up oxygen from the air when we breathe. The heart then pulls the blood back in and sends it out into the arteries. The arteries carry blood to other parts of the body. Our lives depend on the work of our hearts.

There are six supporting sentences in the paragraph. They explain why the writer calls the human heart a hard worker.

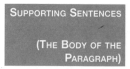

PRACTICE 5.1

Supporting Sentences

Read each paragraph. Follow the directions below it.

1. **Fred's Bad Diet**

Fred has terrible eating habits. He often skips breakfast at home and buys a candy bar at school. For lunch, he usually has french fries, soda, and more candy. In the afternoon, he gets junk food from vending machines. He never eats fresh fruit or vegetables. In the evening, he eats more junk food. Fred needs to make some changes in his diet.

a. Underline the topic sentence and the concluding sentence.

b. Write the number of supporting sentences. _____

c. Complete this statement: The supporting sentences in this

paragraph describe _____

_____

2.

Why I Like Study Groups

I like study groups for several reasons. First of all, studying can be a lonely activity. I feel better when I study with other people. In addition, a study group helps me stay on schedule. When I am alone, I waste time, but with a group, we start on time and focus on our work. Finally, a study group makes me part of a team. I know that many jobs require teamwork, so this is good preparation for my career. For these reasons, I think study groups are a good idea.

a. Underline the topic sentence and the concluding sentence.

b. Write the number of supporting sentences. _____

c. Complete this statement: The supporting sentences in this

paragraph give _____ reasons why _____
   (NUMBER)

_____

3.

How to Annoy a Roommate

It is easy to annoy a roommate. One way is to make a lot of noise. Do this especially when your roommate is sleeping or studying. Another way is to leave a mess on the floor. Drop your clothes and shoes everywhere. Finally, eat smelly food in the room. When you finish, put the dirty dishes on the floor, too. If you follow this advice, you will surely drive your roommate crazy.

a. Underline the topic sentence and the concluding sentence.

b. Write the number of supporting sentences. _____

c. Complete this statement: The supporting sentences in this

paragraph show some _____ ways to _____
   (ADJECTIVE)

_____

PART 2 | Sentence Structure

Simple Sentence Patterns II

In Chapter 4, you learned that simple sentences have one subject-verb combination. You saw simple sentences with these two patterns:

1 subject + 1 **verb**	I **drink** coffee.
2 subjects + 1 **verb**	Matteo and I **drink** coffee.

Here are two more patterns for simple sentences. These patterns also have one subject-verb combination.

1 subject + 2 **verbs**	Rick **sits** and **drinks** coffee.
2 subjects + 2 **verbs**	Rick and Tina **sit** and **drink** coffee.

Rules	Examples
1. Use *and* to add a second subject or verb. Do not use a comma.	**Olga and Anna** are musicians. They **sing and play** the piano.
2. Use *or* to connect two negative verbs. Do not repeat *do/does not* or *am/is/ are not*.	I **do not sing or play** the piano. Anna **is not singing or playing** right now.

PRACTICE 5.2

Simple Sentence Patterns

Work alone or with a partner. Find the verbs and write *V* above them. Find the subjects and write *S* above them.

      S   V   V
1. Minja exercises and eats healthy food.

2. She takes vitamins and does not smoke.

3. She eats fresh vegetables and avoids fast food.

4. Her parents and her brother also eat well and exercise.

5. Minja and her brother work out or swim six days a week.

6. She walks on a treadmill or rides an exercise bicycle.

7. She does not lift weights or run.

8. Minja and her brother look good and feel great.

Walking on a treadmill   Lifting weights

PRACTICE 5.3

Combining Sentences: Three Patterns

Combine the sentences into one simple sentence. Use *and* or *or*. Make any other changes needed.

Example: London is a capital city. Paris is a capital city.

London and Paris are capital cities.

1. Lobsang lives in Nepal. Lobsang works in Kathmandu.

_____

2. Caracas is in Venezuela. Maracaibo is in Venezuela.

_____

3. Ali has English books. Ramón has English books.

_____

4. Myriam plays the guitar. Myriam sings.

_____

5. Most birds have wings and fly. Many insects have wings and fly.

_____

6. Nadia does not watch TV. Nadia does not go to movies.

_____

7. My grandmother does not drive or use computers. My grandfather does not drive or use computers.

_____

8. Laura works hard. She takes few vacations. Peter works hard. He takes few vacations.

_____

PART 3 | Grammar

The Present Progressive

In Chapter 3, you learned about verbs in the simple present tense. Now you will learn about the **present progressive** (also called the _present continuous_).

A present progressive verb has two parts: (1) _am, is_, or _are_ and (2) a **main verb** that ends in _-ing_.

Present Progressive: Affirmative Statements

Singular		
Subject	**_Be_**	**Main Verb**
I	am	
You	are	
He		working.
She	is	
It		
The clock		

Plural		
Subject	**_Be_**	**Main Verb**
We		
You		
They	are	working.
The clocks		

See Appendix D for contractions with am, is, _and_ are.
See Appendix F for spelling rules for verbs ending in -ing.

PRACTICE 5.4

Describing Actions

Match the words and pictures. Write the sentences with present progressive verbs.

a. They are standing.   e. They are shopping.

b. He is shouting.   f. She is writing.

c. She is laughing.   g. They are relaxing.

d. He is studying.   h. She is driving.

c 1. She is laughing.

e 2. _____

b 3. _____

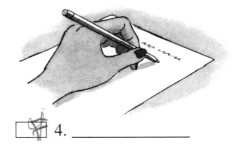

f 4. _____

g 5. _____

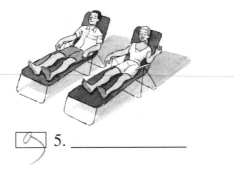

d 6. _____

h 7. _____

a 8. _____

PRACTICE 5.5

Present Progressive: Affirmative

Write the correct present progressive form of the verb in parentheses. (See Appendix F for spelling rules for -*ing* verbs.)

1. (play) Two teams ___are playing___ soccer.

2. (watch) Many people ___Are watching___ the game.

3. (sit) I ___am sitting___ in the stands with my friends.

4. (have) We ___having___ a good time.

5. (run) The players ___are running___ on the field.

6. (pass) One player ___is passing___ the ball.

7. (blow) Now the referee ___is blowing___ her whistle.

8. (make) The people in the stands ___are making___ a lot of noise.

9. (yell) They ___are yelling___ at the referee.

10. (win) My team ___is winning___ this game.

The referee with her whistle

Present Progressive: Negative Statements

Singular			
Subject	**Be**	**Not**	**Main Verb**
I	am		
You	are		
He		not	working.
She	is		
It			
The clock			

Plural			
Subject	**Be**	**Not**	**Main Verb**
We			
You			
They	are	not	working.
The clocks			

See Appendix D for contractions with am, is, *and* are.

PRACTICE 5.6

Present Progressive: Negative

Write the present progressive form of the verb in parentheses. (See Appendix F for spelling rules for *-ing* verbs.)

1. (not, work) Jacinto is on vacation this week. He ___is not working.___

2. (not, rain) It is a beautiful day today. It _____

3. (not, get up) The children are sick, so they are staying in bed today. They _____

4. (not, eat) I am not hungry now, so I _____

5. (not, cry) The baby is happy right now, so he _____ _____

6. (not, make) We are painting the walls carefully. We _____ _____ a mess.

7. (not, die) These plants are healthy. They _____ _____

8. (not, sleep) You are awake. You _____

PRACTICE 5.7

Using the Present Progressive

Work alone or with a partner. Take a piece of paper. Write four or more statements about the people in each picture. Use the present progressive. Include affirmative and negative statements.

Examples: Picture A: The woman is talking to the man. He is not smiling. They are wearing business clothes.

A.   B.

C.

D.

Functions of Present Progressive Verbs

Rules	Examples
1. Use the present progressive for actions happening now, at this moment. 10:21 A.M.	Look out the window. It **is snowing**. Someone **is singing**. Listen!
2. Use the present progressive for actions happening over a longer time in the present. AUG SEPT OCT NOV DEC JAN FEB	He **is taking** math this semester. Ann and Bill **are living** with her parents.
3. Use the present progressive with time expressions such as the following: • *now, right now,* and *at this moment* • *this week, this month, this year*	They are talking on the phone **now**. She is studying English **this year**.
4. Do not use present progressive verbs with adverbs of frequency. Use the simple present.	*go* Sometimes I ~~am going~~ shopping.

PRACTICE 5.8

*Present
Progressive
Versus Simple
Present*

Circle the correct time expression for each sentence.

1. I am working on grammar.	(now)	every day
2. I do my homework.	now	(every day)
3. I am working on page 110.	at this moment	sometimes
4. The teacher is speaking.	at this moment	sometimes
5. The students listen.	now	always
6. Our class meets in room 112.	now	(always)
7. You are thinking.	(right now)	usually
8. You do good work.	right now	(usually)
9. We practice English.	this week	(every day)
10. We are learning about verbs.	this week	every day

Non-Action Verbs

Some verbs do not express action or movement. Do not use these verbs in the present progressive. Use the simple present tense.

> know   does not know
> I ~~am knowing~~ his name, but he ~~is not knowing~~ my name.

Verbs like *know* are called **non-action** verbs (or *verbs with stative meaning*). Other non-action verbs are:

Description	Senses	Mental States	Emotions
be	hear	know	hate
look	see	need	like
seem	smell	want	love

PRACTICE 5.9 Circle the correct verb.

Non-Action Verbs

1. This pizza tastes great. I (am liking / **like**) it!

2. Please be quiet. You (**are making** / make) too much noise.

3. I do not understand the homework. I (am needing / **need**) some help.

4. The students always (are looking / **look**) sleepy on Monday mornings.

5. Beatriz is at the mall. She (**is looking for** / looks for) a new dress.

6. Nanami has her radio on. She (**is listening** / listens) to the news.

7. Listen! Do you hear music? — No, I (am not hearing / **do not hear**) anything.

8. Tom is at the drugstore. He (is wanting / **wants**) some cold medicine.

9. The children are happy in the pool. They (are loving / **love**) the water.

10. We are looking for Ali, but we (**aren't seeing** / don't see) him.

The Verb *Have*

The verb *have* has several meanings. It can be an action verb or a non-action verb.

Rules	Examples
1. You can use the present progressive when *have* means:	
• eating or drinking	He **is having** lunch right now. He always has lunch at noon.
• doing or experiencing something	They **are having** a party this evening. They often have parties.
2. Use the simple present, not the present progressive, when *have* means:	
• possession	*have* They ~~are having~~ a white car.
• relationship	*does not have* She ~~is not having~~ sisters.
• sickness	*has* He ~~is having~~ a cold.

PRACTICE 5.10

Have: Action Versus Non-Action

Circle the correct verb.

1. Slava likes animals, but he (is not having / (does not have)) a pet.

2. Mr. Brown is out of the office right now. He (is having / has) lunch.

3. My sister (is having / has) two children, one boy and one girl.

4. My head hurts, and I (am having / have) a sore throat.

5. Monique (is not having / does not have) long hair.

6. My friends are at a party now. I'm sure they (are having / have) fun.

7. I'm drinking tea, and she (is having / has) coffee.

8. Students often (are having / have) exams at the end of the school year.

PRACTICE 5.11

Editing: Verb Errors

Work alone or with a partner. Find and correct the nine errors in present progressive and simple present verbs. The first error is corrected for you.

         He **wants**   *has*   *s*

Danny ~~is wanting~~ to buy a car. He is having a new job and needing

a car for work. Right now, he is at Ace Used Cars. He is looking at a

car. A salesperson is talk to Danny. She describing the car to him. He

listens to her. The car is not bad, but Danny is not liking it very much.

He is want a nice car, but he is not having much money. The price for

this car seems right. He is thinking about it.

PRACTICE 5.12

Using Present Progressive and Simple Present

Work alone or with a partner. Take a piece of paper. Look at the photos on pages 1, 27, and 97. Choose one photo.

A. Use your imagination. Write four or more facts about the people in your photo. Use **simple present** verbs.

Example: Page 6   The man's name **is** Rey.
He **speaks** Spanish and English.
He **has** a new job.
He **plays** basketball after work.

B. Write four or more sentences describing the actions in your photo. Use **present progressive** verbs.

Example: Page 6   Rey **is** smiling.
He **is not talking.**
He **is looking** at me.
He **is wearing** a suit.

PART 4 | The Writing Process

Your Paragraph: *What Is Happening in This Photo?*

You are going to write a paragraph about what you see happening in a photo, like the model paragraphs on page 98.

Step 1: Prewrite

a. Work with a partner. Look at the four photos on the next page. Match one or more adjectives in the box to the people in each photo.

angry	happy	relaxed	upset
excited	nervous	scared	worried

b. Choose one of the four photos to write about. You and your partner must choose different photos. Ask your partner questions about his or her photo. For example, ask:

Who are the people in the photo? Where are they?
What are they doing? What are they wearing? How do they feel?

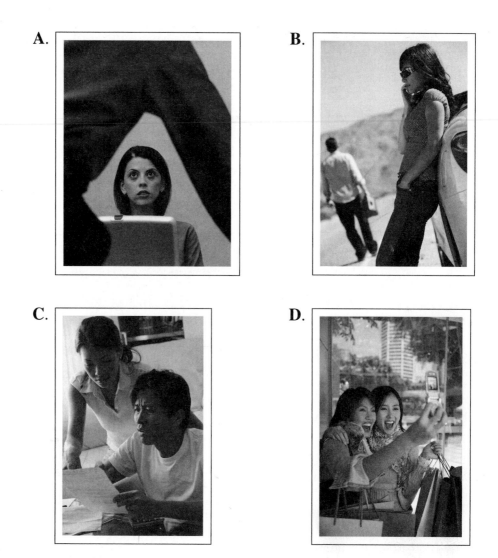

A.

B.

C.

D.

c. Take notes about your photo. Include one or more adjectives to describe the feelings of the people.

Step 2: Write

a. Use your notes to write the first draft of a paragraph. At the beginning of your paragraph, do two things: (1) Identify which photo you are writing about, and (2) state the main idea of your paragraph. You can do this in one or two sentences. Look at the models on page 98 for examples.

b. Continue writing your first draft. Make sure that your supporting sentences show why your main idea is true. Give your paragraph a title.

Step 3: Edit

a. Read your paragraph again. It may help you to read it out loud. Make changes if needed.

b. Edit your paper carefully. Check for mistakes before you show it to anyone.

c. Peer review: Exchange papers with a partner. Follow the Reviewer's Checklist below. Check (✓) each box when you finish that step.

Reviewer's Checklist — Chapter 5

Your partner's name: _____

<u>Content</u>
☐ Read all of your partner's paragraph.
☐ Underline any part of the paragraph you do not understand. Ask your partner to explain it.
☐ Circle the writer's main idea about the photo.
☐ Ask questions if you want more information.

<u>Form</u>
Look at these parts of your partner's paper. Mark any problems on the paper in pencil. Put a question mark (?) if you are not sure about something.

☐ the title   ☐ the use of simple present verbs
☐ capital letters and periods   ☐ the use of present progressive
☐ a subject in every sentence   verbs

---

d. Return your partner's paper. Say something nice about the paragraph, such as "Good work" or "It's a good start."

e. Look at your own paper. If you do not agree with a comment on it, then ask another student or your teacher.

Step 4: Write the Final Draft

a. On your first draft, mark any changes you want to make. Then take another piece of paper and write a new draft.

b. Edit your paragraph carefully. Then hand it in to your teacher.

Results of the Writing Process

Your teacher will give you feedback on your paragraph. Look carefully at the comments and marks on the paper. Ask your teacher about anything you do not understand. Your teacher may ask you to write a new draft.

Edit your new draft carefully before you hand it in. Remember to hand in your old and new drafts together, with the new draft on top.

When you do not need to rewrite a paragraph anymore, put it in your folder.

Expansion Activities

Your Journal

Continue making entries in your journal. If you need a topic for a journal entry, these ideas might help:

- Where are you at this moment? Describe what you are doing and what you are wearing. Are there any other people around you? Tell what they are doing.
- Name a job that interests you, one that you might like to do in the future. Why are you interested in this job?
- Do you watch TV? If you do, tell when, where, and what you watch. If you do not watch TV, tell why not.
- What do you do for exercise? Do you exercise every day, sometimes, or never?
- These days, you are going to classes and you are using this book. What else are you doing — in school and out — to learn English? What helps you the most?

Challenge: *My Own Photo*

Choose a magazine photo of people, or choose a photo of your family or friends. Try to choose a photo of people doing something, not simply looking at the camera. Review the questions under Step 1 on page 113. Take notes about your photo.

Use your notes to write the first draft of a paragraph. Describe what the people are doing and wearing. Give your paragraph a title.

Ask a friend or a classmate to look at your photo and to review your first draft. Use the Reviewer's Checklist on page 115. Prepare a final draft. Then give your paper and your photo to your teacher.

Your Hometown

Where is your hometown?

Chapter Preview

Part 1: Organization
Topic Sentences and Supporting Sentences II

Part 2: Grammar
There Is and *There Are*
A, *An*, and *The*

Part 3: Vocabulary and Sentence Structure
Prepositions for Describing Location
Prepositional Phrases in Sentences

Part 4: The Writing Process
Your Paragraph: *Describing My Hometown*
Results of the Writing Process

Expansion Activities

Chapter Preview

Work with a partner or in a small group. Read the model paragraphs. Answer the questions that follow.

MODEL
Paragraph 1

My Hometown

I am from Canóvanas, Puerto Rico. It is a small city with a big heart. It is in the northeastern part of Puerto Rico. There are about 30,000 people there. They are not rich, and their houses are small. There are good people in Canóvanas. My neighbors are like my family. When there is a problem, people are always ready to help. That is the best thing about my hometown. I miss the friendly people of Canóvanas.

MODEL
Paragraph 2

A Special City

Almaty, my hometown, is a special city. It is in the southeastern part of Kazakhstan, near China. The name *Almaty* means "the apple place." The first apples in the world grew in that area. My hometown is the cultural center of Kazakhstan. It has wonderful theaters and museums. Also, Almaty has the world's largest speed-skating rink. It is in the beautiful mountains outside the city. Today, Almaty is no longer the capital of Kazakhstan, but it is still a special city.

Questions about model paragraph 1:

1. The topic and the controlling idea are in the first two sentences. Copy them on the line below. Circle the topic and underline the controlling idea.

   _____

2. How small is Canóvanas? It has about _____ people.

3. Copy a sentence that supports the idea that Canóvanas has "a big heart."

   _____

4. Complete these sentences from the paragraph.

    a. They are not rich, and _____ houses are small.

    b. _____ are good people in Canóvanas.

    c. When _____ is a problem, people are always ready to help.

5. Look at sentences 4a, b, and c. Then complete these statements. Write *there* or *their*.

    a. Use _____ + a noun to show possession (like *my, your, his, her, its,* and *our*).

    b. Use _____ + *is* or *are* to introduce new information.

Questions about model paragraph 2:

1. What is the topic sentence? Copy it on the line below. Circle the topic and underline the controlling idea.

    _____

2. Where is Almaty? _____

3. Why does the writer think that Almaty is special? List three reasons.

    _____

    _____

    _____

A speed skater inside a skating rink

4. Write the prepositions used in these sentences from the paragraph.

    a. It is _____ the southeastern part _____ Kazakhstan, _____ China.

    b. It is _____ the beautiful mountains _____ the city.

You will write a paragraph describing your hometown later in this chapter (page 132).

PART 1 | Organization

Topic Sentences and Supporting Sentences II

Support for the Topic Sentence

In Chapter 3, you learned about topic sentences. In Chapter 5, you learned about supporting sentences. They form the body of a paragraph. They show why the controlling idea in the topic sentence is true. They present **evidence** — information to prove a point.

PRACTICE 6.1

Supporting a Topic Sentence

Work with a partner or in a small group. Read the paragraph. Then follow the directions below.

My Best Friend's Room

My best friend's room is very neat. Her desk always looks clean and organized. There are only a few books and her laptop on it. She always puts her clothes away. There are never any clothes on the floor or on her bed. She also makes her bed every day. It always looks perfect. I wish my room looked like her room.

1. Underline the topic sentence. Circle the controlling idea.

2. What evidence supports the topic sentence? List three details.

_____

_____

_____

3. Underline the concluding sentence. What does it mean?

Paragraph Unity

All the supporting sentences in a paragraph must be **relevant** — they must relate to the main idea. For example, look at the three sentences on the next page. Only one of the sentences is relevant to the paragraph

"My Best Friend's Room" in Practice 6.1. You could add this sentence to the paragraph. Which one is it? The other two sentences are **irrelevant** — not directly related to the main idea of the paragraph.

(1) Her hair is always neat, too.

(2) There are two large windows in her room.

(3) She puts her pens and papers away in the drawers.

Sentence (1) is irrelevant because the paragraph is about her room only. It is not about her hair or any other part of her life. Sentence (2) is also irrelevant. It does nothing to support the main idea. Sentence (3) is the only relevant sentence. It tells how she keeps her desk neat. It supports the main idea.

Read the following paragraph. Two irrelevant sentences are crossed out. Why are they irrelevant?

My Favorite Holiday

I always loved the traditions of New Year's Eve in my country. First, we all cleaned our homes so they looked nice for the new year. We also put up colored lights and other decorations. Then everyone dressed up in nice new clothes. ~~My brother never wanted to dress up or help with the cleaning.~~ The best part was a special dinner with my whole family. Then at midnight, everyone went outside, and there were fireworks in the streets. ~~Sometimes we had fireworks on other holidays, too.~~ New Year's Eve was always an exciting night in my country.

The writer's topic is New Year's Eve in her home country. Her paragraph describes the holiday traditions that she loved. The sentence about her brother is irrelevant because it does not describe a tradition that she loved. The sentence about fireworks on other holidays is not about New Year's Eve, so that is also irrelevant.

PRACTICE 6.2

Identifying Irrelevant Sentences

Work alone or with a partner. Read each paragraph. Underline the topic sentence. Find two irrelevant sentences, and cross them out.

1.

Roberto

My friend Roberto is a kind person. He helps everybody in his family. He drives his mother to the doctor or the store. He helps her understand English. People speak Spanish in Mexico. He checks his little brothers' homework. He also plays baseball with them. Roberto is a good soccer player, too. He listens to his sisters' problems. He gives them good advice. Roberto is a good son and a good brother.

2.

Hot-Air Balloons

It is easy to understand how a hot-air balloon works. Airplanes are harder to understand. A gas burner heats the air inside the balloon. The hot air is lighter than the air outside, so the balloon rises. When the burner is turned down, the air inside the balloon cools off. Then the balloon starts going down. That is how a hot-air balloon works. Two men in France took the first hot-air balloon ride in 1783.

3.

The Petersons' Farm

The Peterson family is having an excellent year on their farm. Their vegetables are growing very well this summer. The corn is tall, and the tomato plants are full of tomatoes. Corn and tomatoes have many uses. All the Petersons' animals are in good health. Their hens are producing many eggs. The young sheep are growing quickly. You can make good cheese from sheep's milk. Every day, customers stop at the farm to buy vegetables and eggs. Business is good, and the Petersons are happy.

4.   **Conditions in Antarctica**

Antarctica is a difficult and dangerous place for people. Penguins live there. It is very cold, with the average temperature about 40 degrees below zero. The air is very dry, and there are strong winds. In the winter, the sun never comes up. I would never go there in the winter. In the summer, the sun's rays are bad for people's skin and eyes. They need protection from both the cold and the sun. Some scientists stay there to work for a few weeks or months, but no one calls Antarctica home.

PART 2 | Grammar

There Is and *There Are*

Sentences with *there is* and *there are* often introduce new information.

> Under line: There is **a lot of work to do!**

In addition, sentences with *there is* and *there are* often:

- tell the time of something

    There is **a train** to the city **at 7:30 A.M.**

- tell where someone or something is

    There are good **restaurants** of many kinds **in my hometown.**

Affirmative Statements with *There Is* and *There Are*

There	*Is*	Singular/ Noncount Noun	
There	is	a lake	near here.
		mail	on the table.

There	*Are*	Plural Noun	
There	are	many things	to do.
		four people	in my family.

See Appendix C for information about singular, plural, and noncount nouns.

Rules	Examples
1. Use *there is/are* + *no* + noun to form a negative statement.	**There is no** elevator in this building. **There are no** tall buildings in my city. **There is no** food in the refrigerator.
2. Do not confuse *there are* with *they are*. • Use *there are* to introduce a new subject. • Use *they* instead of repeating a noun.	**There are** <u>two women</u> named Amina in my class. The two women are *They are* from Somalia.
3. Do not confuse *there* with *their*. • Use *there* + *is* or *are*. • Use *their* + a noun. *Their* shows possession.	**There** <u>are</u> five people in the group. Those are my friends. **Their** <u>names</u> are Isabel and Pilar.

PRACTICE 6.3

There Is *Versus* There Are

Complete the sentences. Write *there is* or *there are*.

(1) __There are__ many shopping malls in North America, but the West Edmonton Mall in Canada is the biggest. (2) _____ more than 800 stores in the mall. A visitor to the mall can shop for days. (3) _____ many other things to do, too. For example, (4) _____ a skating rink, (5) _____ many amusement park rides, and (6) _____ a theater with eight movie screens. (7) _____ twenty restaurants for hungry shoppers, and (8) _____ even a hotel. (9) _____ something for everyone at the West Edmonton Mall.

PRACTICE 6.4

There, They, *or* Their

Circle the correct word.

1. (a) (There / They) are two students from Korea in my class.
   (b) (There / Their) names are Jun Seong and Min Sup. They usually sit over there.

2. (a) (There / They) are about 100 students in this program.
   (b) (There / They) are from different countries. (c) (There / They) are learning English.

3. The teachers often meet on Wednesdays. (a) (There / Their) meetings take place in the conference room. (b) (There / Their) is a large round table in there. They usually have (c) (there / their) lunch during the meetings.

PRACTICE 6.5

Using **There Is** *and* **There Are**

Take a piece of paper. Answer the questions below. Write complete sentences with *there is* and *there are*.

Example: Are there many plants in your bedroom?
No, there are no plants in my bedroom.

1. How many floors are there in the building where you live?
2. Is there a map of the world in your classroom?
3. How many desks are there in your classroom?
4. Is there a swimming pool at your school?
5. How many people are in your family?
6. Are there pictures in your wallet?

A, An, and *The*

The words *a, an,* and *the* are **articles**. Articles often come before nouns.

Using *A* and *An*

Rules	Examples
1. Use *a* and *an* with singular nouns. • Use *a* before a consonant sound. • Use *an* before a vowel sound. (Think about the first sound — not the first letter — of the noun.)	**a b**ridge, **a ch**ild, **a h**ouse, **a u**niversity **an a**pple, **an e**gg, **an h**our, **an u**mbrella
2. Do not use *a* or *an* with plural or noncount nouns.	I have ~~a~~ books. I have ~~a~~ money.
3. Use *a* or *an* when: • the noun is not specific • the noun is first introduced	I need **an** <u>eraser</u>. (Any eraser — I do not care which eraser.) There is **a** <u>bank</u> on Green Street.
4. One or more adjectives can come between an article and a noun.	an <u>old</u> man a <u>new</u>, <u>red</u> truck

See Appendix C for information about singular, plural, and noncount nouns.
See Appendix J for information about adjectives before nouns.

PRACTICE 6.6

A, An, or No Article in Definitions

Write *a* or *an*, or put a dash (—), meaning "no article."

1. Bolivia is _a_ country.
2. Cats are — animals.
3. _a_ mouse is _an_ animal.
4. Blue is _a_ color.
5. _a_ jet is _an_ airplane.
6. _an_ inn is _a_ small hotel.
7. *Small* is _an_ adjective.
8. *Come* and *go* are _—_ verbs.
9. A dollar is _—_ money.
10. Texas is _an_ American state.
11. Rome and Milan are _—_ Italian cities.
12. _a_ skyscraper is _a_ very tall building.
13. _an_ ant is _an_ insect.
14. Jaguars and Mercedes are _—_ expensive cars.

PRACTICE 6.7

Using A and An in Definitions

Work alone or with a partner. Write definitions for the words in parentheses. Use the words in the box. Use *a* or *an* as needed.

animal	city	country	insect	language

Ants, bees, and mosquitoes are insects.

1. (Buenos Aires) _Buenos Aires is a city._
2. (India) _____
3. (a horse) _____
4. (English) _____
5. (a bee) _____
6. (an elephant) _____
7. (Mexico) _____
8. (Japanese) _____
9. (Baghdad) _____
10. (a mosquito) _____
11. (Syria) _____
12. (Cairo) _____

Using *The*

Rules	Examples
1. Use *the* with singular, plural, or noncount nouns.	**the** sun **the** stars **the** weather
2. Use *the* when the noun means a specific person, place, or thing.	Specific: I know all **the students** in my class. Not specific: **Students** go to school.
3. Use *the* when you repeat a noun already introduced.	There is **a** <u>bank</u> on Green Street. You can get cash at **the** <u>bank</u>.

PRACTICE 6.8

A, An, or The

Complete the sentences. Write *a, an,* or *the*.

1. We have __a__ new baby in our family. __the__ baby's name
   a.   b.

   is Niko. He is __the__ first child for my brother and sister-in-law.
               c.

   They do not have __a__ daughter.
                     d.

2. __an__ aquarium is __the__ building where people can see fish and
   a.   b.

   other sea animals. My hometown has __a__ new aquarium.
                                        c.

   __an__ aquarium in my hometown is very interesting.
   d.

3. Lee works in __the__ large department store. __a__ store is on
                a.   b.

   Market Street. He is __a__ salesclerk at __the__ store.
                        c.   d.

4. They are building __an__ airport near my city. There is __an__ old
                      a.   b.

   airport, too, but it is small. __the__ new airport will be big.
                                  c.

5. I am from Jakarta. It is __a__ capital of Indonesia. It is on
                            a.

   __the__ northwest coast of Java. Java is __an__ island.
   b.   c.

PART 3 | Vocabulary and Sentence Structure

Prepositions for Describing Location

In Chapter 4, you learned about prepositions. A preposition can be one word, such as *to, from,* or *after,* or more than one word, such as *in front of* or *in back of.*

Prepositions have many uses. They often help describe **location** — where someone or something is.

Honduras is **in** Central America.

It is **between** Guatemala and Nicaragua.

It is **next to** El Salvador. It is **near** Belize.

The northern part of Honduras is **on** the Caribbean Sea. A small part **in** the south is **on** the Pacific Ocean.

PRACTICE 6.9

Recognizing Prepositions

Circle the ten prepositions in this paragraph. The first one is circled for you.

I love visiting my grandparents. They live (on) a farm in a small town in Turkey. It is near the Black Sea. There is a big garden next to their house. My grandparents grow vegetables and herbs in the garden. There is a small barn in back of the house. The goats and chickens sleep in the barn. There are many apple trees in front of the house. The farm is a beautiful place in the spring and summer.

Using *In, On,* and *At* to Describe Location

Rules	Examples
1. Use *in* + a continent, country, state, province, or city.	Canada is **in North America**. There are ten provinces **in Canada**. The beautiful city of Vancouver is **in British Columbia**. My friend Brian lives **in Vancouver**.
2. Use *on* + a street (without a specific address) or a floor of a building.	Their building is **on King Street**. We are meeting **on the tenth floor**.
3. Use *at* + a specific address or building.	The Kelleys live **at 132 King Street**. He works **at the hospital**.

PRACTICE 6.10

In, On, and At *for Location*

Complete the sentences with *in, on,* or *at*.

1. Nina lives _____ California.

2. California is _____ the United States.

3. She lives _____ Water Street _____ San Francisco.

4. Her building is _____ 94 Water Street.

5. Her apartment is _____ the second floor.

6. She works _____ the Orchard Hotel.

7. The hotel is _____ Bush Street.

8. The entrance is _____ 665 Bush Street.

PRACTICE 6.11

In, On, and At *in Personal Information*

Complete the sentences. Write about yourself.

1. I live **in** _____

2. My hometown is **in** _____

3. I live **on** _____

4. My home is **at** _____

Prepositional Phrases in Sentences

In Chapter 4, you learned that a preposition and a noun form a prepositional phrase. A writer can put a prepositional phrase in several places in a sentence.

Rules	Examples
Prepositional phrases can come: • after *be* • after other verbs • after nouns • at the beginning or end of sentences	Dakar <u>is</u> **in Senegal**. Miguel <u>comes</u> **from Mexico City**. The <u>weather</u> **in India** is usually hot. **In my country**, there are beautiful forests. There are beautiful forests **in my country**.

Use a comma after a prepositional phrase at the beginning of a sentence. The subject and verb follow.

S   V
In my hometown, the public gardens are full of flowers.

PRACTICE 6.12	Underline the prepositional phrases in the examples on the right. Then match the rules and the examples. Write the letters.
Recognizing Prepositional Phrases	

RULES   EXAMPLES

_c_ 1. *be* + prepositional phrase   a. The animals on these islands
                                              are unusual.

___ 2. other verb + prepositional   b. Many visitors travel to the
          phrase   islands.

___ 3. noun + prepositional phrase   c. The Galápagos Islands are
                                              <u>in the Pacific Ocean</u>.

___ 4. prepositional phrase at the   d. I hope to visit the islands
          beginning of a sentence   in the future.

___ 5. prepositional phrase at the   e. In the Galápagos, the
          end of a sentence   animals are protected.

PRACTICE 6.13	Work alone or with a partner. Take a piece of paper. Look at the map of Cambodia. Write six or more sentences about places on the map. Use *between, in, near, next to,* and *on*.
Using Prepositional Phrases	

Example: Cambodia is next to Thailand.

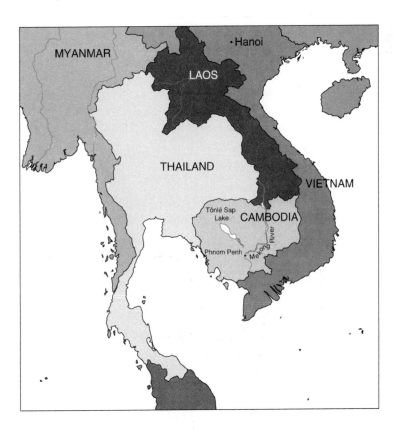

PART 4 | The Writing Process

Your Paragraph: *Describing My Hometown*

You are going to write a paragraph about your hometown, like the model paragraphs on page 118.

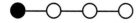

Step 1: Prewrite

a. Get ready to write by **brainstorming**. Brainstorming is a way of getting ideas. It means thinking about a topic and quickly making a list of all the words and phrases that come to mind.

- Do not write complete sentences. Just take notes.
- Do not worry about the order of your ideas. You will put them in order later.

Here are the notes from one student's brainstorming:

> In Kazakhstan, in the southeast, near China (how far?)
>
> big city – population??   noisy (but I like)   public transportation good
>
> some beautiful buildings   culture!
>
> mountains, beautiful nature, snow
>
> Medeo – high in mountains, rink for speed skating – famous
>
> expensive city   was capital city (when?)
>
> name = "the apple place"   (Kazakhstan famous for apples)

Now brainstorm about your hometown. Take notes.

b. Work with a partner. Ask your partner questions about his or her hometown:

Where are you from? Where is it? What is it like? What is special about it?

Answer your partner's questions about your hometown. If you get more ideas, add them to your notes.

c. Review your notes to prepare for your paragraph. Decide what information you do and do not want to use.

d. Look again at the notes from page 132. The writer has made changes. She has decided on a title. She has written a topic sentence. She has crossed out irrelevant information.

Almaty

topic sentence: Almaty, my hometown, is a special city.

In Kazakhstan, in the southeast, near China ~~(how far?)~~

~~big city — population??~~   ~~noisy (but I like)~~   ~~public transportation good~~

~~some beautiful buildings~~   culture! (theaters, museums)

mountains, beautiful nature, snow

Medeo — high in mountains, rink for speed skating — famous   World's

   largest

~~expensive city~~   was capital city before ~~(when?)~~

name = "the apple place" (Kazakhstan famous for apples) first apples

                                              in the world

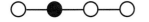 **Step 2: Write**

Use your notes to write your first draft. Begin your paragraph with a topic sentence. See the models on page 118 for examples. Remember, your supporting sentences must relate to your topic sentence.

Writer's Tip

Prewriting often helps a writer decide on a topic sentence. However, some writers like to do a first draft of a paragraph without a topic sentence. Then they add it. Also, writers sometimes change their topic sentence when they edit.

○—○—●—○ **Step 3: Edit**

 a. Read your paragraph again. It may help you to read it out loud. Make changes if needed.

 b. Edit your paper carefully. Check for mistakes before you show it to anyone.

 c. Peer review: Exchange papers with a partner. Follow the Reviewer's Checklist below. Check (✓) each box when you finish that step.

Reviewer's Checklist — Chapter 6

Your partner's name: _____

Content

☐ Read all of your partner's paragraph.

☐ Underline any part of the paragraph you do not understand. Ask your partner to explain it.

☐ Circle the topic sentence. Write *TS* on the paper if there is no topic sentence.

☐ Read the supporting sentences again. Ask questions if you want more information.

Form

Look at these parts of your partner's paper. Mark any problems on the paper in pencil. Put a question mark (?) if you are not sure about something.

☐ the format of the paper — heading, title, margins, spacing

☐ a subject in every sentence

☐ a verb for every subject

☐ the use of *there is* and *there are*

☐ the use of prepositions

---

 d. Return your partner's paper. Say something nice about it, such as "I liked reading about your hometown" or "Good first draft."

 e. Look at your own paper. If you do not agree with a comment on it, then ask another student or your teacher.

○—○—○—● **Step 4: Write the Final Draft**

a. On your first draft, mark any changes you want to make. Then take another piece of paper and write a new draft.

b. Edit your new draft carefully. Then hand it in to your teacher.

Results of the Writing Process

Your teacher will give you feedback on your paragraph. Look carefully at your teacher's comments and marks on the paper. Ask your teacher about anything you do not understand. Your teacher may ask you to write a new draft.

Edit your new draft carefully before you hand it in. Remember to hand in your old and new drafts together, with the new draft on top.

When you do not need to rewrite a paragraph anymore, put it in your folder.

Expansion Activities

Your Journal

Continue making entries in your journal. If you cannot think of a topic for a journal entry, try one of these ideas:

- Do you ever see the sun come up? Do you ever watch it set? Describe a place where you like to watch the sunrise or sunset.
- Go to a public place and do some people-watching. Choose a person, and describe him or her. What does the person look like? How old is he or she? What is the person doing? What is he or she wearing?
- Do you carry a wallet, a purse, or a backpack? Describe what is in it right now, or describe the things you usually carry and tell why.
- Describe a nice place to visit in your country. It could be a famous place, such as a city or national park, or a place that few people know about.
- Write about using English outside of class. Who do you talk to in English? When do you listen to English or read it?

Challenge: *A Favorite Place*

Write a paragraph about a favorite place. For example, you could describe your favorite room at home or a place where you like to go. Before you begin, brainstorm about the place (as you did for the prewriting activity on page 132). Then review your notes.

Use your notes to write your first draft. Begin your paragraph with a topic sentence. All the supporting sentences should relate to your main idea.

Ask a friend or a classmate to review your first draft. Use the Reviewer's Checklist on page 134. Then prepare a final draft and give it to your teacher.

Remembering an Important Day

A big day

Chapter Preview

Part 1: Organization
Organizing Your Ideas

Part 2: Sentence Structure and Mechanics
Compound Sentences
Using Commas

Part 3: Grammar and Vocabulary
The Simple Past

Part 4: The Writing Process
Your Paragraph: *An Important Day*
Results of the Writing Process

Expansion Activities

Chapter Preview

Work with a partner or in a small group. Read the model paragraphs. Answer the questions that follow.

MODEL

Paragraph 1

An Important Day in My Life

The day of my high school graduation was a good day for me. It was a Saturday. In the morning, I got dressed. I had a new suit and tie for that day. Then I went to a friend's house. Six of my friends were there. Later, we rode to the school together in my friend's car. At 2:00 P.M., all the students in my class entered the hall. My parents and grandparents were inside the hall, and they took many pictures. The principal called the names of the honor students first. I was in that group, and I won a prize because I was the best math student. My family was proud of me that day.

MODEL

Paragraph 2

My Wedding Day

I have many wonderful memories of my wedding day. I would like to tell you about three of them. First of all, I remember the beautiful weather. The week before was cold and cloudy, but my wedding day was sunny and warm. I felt lucky. I also remember seeing smiles all around me that day. Almost 100 of my relatives and friends were there. They liked my future husband, so they were happy for me. Most of all, I remember walking down the aisle with him. I carried a bouquet of yellow flowers, and I held his arm tightly. My heart was very full. This unforgettable day began a new life for me.

Questions about model paragraph 1:

1. What is the topic sentence? Copy it on the line below. Circle the topic and underline the controlling idea.

_____

2. What details does the writer include in his description of the day?

☐ the weather   ☐ other people   ☐ his clothing

☐ places   ☐ things that he did   ☐ his feelings

3. Give one reason why it was a good day for the writer.

_____

4. What words and phrases help show that the writer is using time order? Write three of them here: _____, _____, and _____

5. Complete these sentences from the paragraph with the **simple past** forms of the verb *be*.

a. It _____ a Saturday.

b. Six of my friends _____ there.

6. Complete these sentences from the paragraph with the **simple past** forms of **regular verbs**.

a. At 2:00 P.M., all the students in my class _____ the hall.

b. The principal _____ the names of the honor students first.

7. Complete these sentences from the paragraph with the **simple past** forms of **irregular verbs**.

a. In the morning, I _____ dressed.

b. Then I _____ to a friend's house.

Questions about model paragraph 2:

1. The topic and the controlling idea are in the first two sentences. Copy them on the lines below. Circle the topic and underline the controlling idea.

_____

_____

2. What three memories of her wedding day does the writer focus on?

☐ the weather   ☑ the people at her wedding

☐ the way she looked   ☐ the place she got married

☐ the music   ☐ the way she felt

3. What adjective means "impossible to forget"? _____

4. Complete these sentences with the **coordinating conjunctions** the writer used.

a. The week before was cloudy, _____ my wedding day was sunny and warm.

b. They liked my husband, _____ they were happy for me.

c. I carried a bouquet of yellow flowers, _____ I held his arm tightly.

You will write a paragraph describing an important day in your life later in this chapter (page 156).

PART 1 | Organization

Organizing Your Ideas

The information in a paragraph needs to be organized. The writer must put the information in order. This makes the paragraph easier to read and understand.

There are many ways to organize a paragraph. For example, you can use time order. You studied time order in Chapter 4. Model paragraph 1 on page 138 uses time order. Model paragraph 2, however, is different. Read how the two writers organized their ideas.

Model Paragraph 1: Getting Organized

For a prewriting activity, the writer of model paragraph 1 on page 138 did some brainstorming. He made a list of notes about the day.

thinking idea

got up
had breakfast
made phone calls
got dressed – new clothes
→ T's house – 6 friends
drive around town, drive to school
walking into hall with my class
parents, grandparents, pictures
honor students first, my prize
dinner at restaurant
parties

Parties too

The writer needed to limit his paragraph. He had to decide what information from his list to keep and what information to leave out.

PRACTICE 7.1

Organizing Ideas from Prewriting

Work alone or with a partner. Reread model paragraph 1 on page 138. In the list of notes above, underline the details that the writer chose for his paragraph. Cross out the other notes.

Model Paragraph 2: Getting Organized

The writer of model paragraph 2 on page 138 also needed to limit her paragraph. She could not give all the details of her wedding day. She had to decide what to include and what to leave out.

As a prewriting activity, this writer tried **freewriting**. Freewriting means writing without stopping for five or ten minutes. You keep your pen or pencil moving across the page. You do not worry about spelling, grammar, or complete sentences. You can use words in your first language if you do not know the words in English. You write as fast as you can.

Here is the freewriting that the writer of model paragraph 2 did.

> My wedding day — one of most important days of my life —
> I have many things to say. Exciting, wonderful day. The day
> beautiful, warm sun, a surprise — not like before. It was
> October, a Saturday. In the early morning, I woke up before the
> ring of my alarm clock. I was excited. I start to get ready, doing
> my hair, my dress — what will I say about my dress? — my
> sisters and my friends in my room helping me. At the church,
> I remember flowers and music — singing, piano. Feeling love
> around me. Many friends, relatives — almost 100 — I see their
> faces, everybody smiling and smiling, so happy for me. I see my
> future husband — our eyes meeting. About the wedding — the
> (name?) talking, he gave much good advice to us. I walked (how
> to say?) with my husband, I remember walking slowly, holding his
> arm so tightly, so happy. Beginning of our new life together.

PRACTICE 7.2

Organizing Ideas from Prewriting

Reread model paragraph 2 on page 138. Then look at the writer's freewriting above. Underline the parts of her freewriting that she decided to use for her paragraph.

The writer of model paragraph 2 decided not to use time order in her paragraph. She chose **listing order**. She lists three important memories of her wedding day — the lovely weather, the smiles of her friends and relatives, and the walk down the aisle with her husband — and she gives details about each one.

PRACTICE 7.3

Adding Details

Look again at model paragraph 2 on page 138. Compare it with the freewriting above. Look for details in the paragraph that were not in her notes. On page 138, underline the new details.

PART 2 | Sentence Structure and Mechanics

Compound Sentences

Simple Versus Compound Sentences

In Chapters 4 and 5, you learned about simple sentences. You studied four patterns for simple sentences. Each pattern has one subject-verb combination.

1 subject + 1 **verb**	Emi **loves** music.
2 subjects + 1 **verb**	Emi and **her friends love** music.
1 subject + 2 **verbs**	They **listen** to music and **watch** music videos.
2 subjects + 2 **verbs**	She and **her friends love** music and often **go** to concerts.

A **compound sentence** is another kind of sentence. It has two subject-verb combinations, as in this example:

    1   2

Emi **loves** music, **and** her friends **love** music, too.

To make a compound sentence, connect two simple sentences. Put a comma after the first simple sentence, and then put a **coordinating conjunction** such as *and, but,* or *so.*

PRACTICE 7.4

Recognizing Compound Sentences

Find the four compound sentences in the paragraph. In each one, mark the subjects *S* and the verbs *V*. Also, circle the comma and coordinating conjunction. The first compound sentence has been done for you.

Mt. Kilimanjaro in Tanzania, East Africa

Climbing Mt. Kilimanjaro is difficult
but possible. The mountain is 5,895
meters high, and snow covers the top
of it. Climbers need warm clothes and
good boots but no special climbing
skills. The trip is 50 to 60 miles
long, and it usually takes several days.
Problems can occur, so it is important to
go with a guide. (Your guide should be a person who knows the
mountain well.) It is also important to be healthy and in good physical
condition. The climb is hard work, but the views from the top are
wonderful.

And, But, and So in Compound Sentences

The coordinating conjunctions *and, but,* and *so* have different meanings.

Rules	Examples
1. Use *and* to add information.	Max is a bus driver, **and** he works in Montreal.
2. Use *but* when the second idea is different or surprising.	He works in the city, **but** he does not live in the city.
3. Use *so* to show a result.	He is nice and friendly, **so** his passengers and co-workers like him.

See Appendix K for more information about coordinating conjunctions.

PRACTICE 7.5

Coordinating Conjunctions

Circle the correct coordinating conjunction.

1. It was a beautiful place, (and / but) I was happy there.

2. Hee Eun did not study for the test, (but / so) she got a good grade.

3. I liked the movie, (and / but) I did not understand all of it.

4. First, I cleaned the kitchen, (and / so) then I cleaned the bathroom.

5. It rained all day, (but / so) they did not play baseball.

6. The music was great, (and / but) there was free food.

7. Their apartment building is nice, (but / so) that part of the city is not.

8. The shoes did not fit right, (but / so) I did not buy them.

PRACTICE 7.6

Creating Compound Sentences

Combine each pair of simple sentences into a compound sentence. Use the coordinating conjunction in parentheses.

1. Last year, my son was six years old. My daughter was four. (and)

   Last year, my son was six years old, and my

   daughter was four.

2. One day, my children were at home. My friend's little boy was there, too. (and)

   _____

3. The children were in the kitchen. I was not with them. (but)

   _____

4. My friend's son picked up the phone. He called 911. (and)

   _____

5. He did not talk to the operator. She knew our phone number and address. (but)

   _____

6. She believed that we had an emergency. She sent the police to our house. (so)

_____

7. There was no emergency. The police officers were angry. (so)

_____

8. I was upset with the children. I had a serious talk with them. (so)

_____

9. It was just a child's mistake. I had to pay a $50 fine. (but)

_____

10. I learned a lesson. The children did, too. (and)

_____

Using Commas

On pages 143 and 144, you learned about using commas in compound sentences. Here are four more rules for using commas.

Rules	Examples
1. Use a comma between the date and the year.	He was born on July **1, 1955**.
2. Use a comma after a time expression or a time-order word at the beginning of a sentence. (Exception: Do not use a comma after *Then*.)	**Yesterday morning,** I got up early. **First,** I took a shower and got dressed. **After that,** I had breakfast. **Then** I brushed my teeth.
3. Use a comma between items in a series of words or phrases.	You, Tomasz, Sara, and I are in one group. The students wrote their final drafts, checked them, and handed them in.
4. Do not use a comma when you connect only two words or phrases.	Mike **and** all his friends were at the game. I did not see Luis **or** call him.

PRACTICE 7.7

Adding Commas

The following sentences are missing twelve commas. Add commas as needed. Some sentences need no commas.

1. I was born on June 16 1988.

2. My parents were born in 1956.

3. In August of 2006 we had a big family reunion.

4. My parents invited all our relatives and everyone came to our house for the day.

5. My grandparents aunts uncles and cousins brought many kinds of food.

6. We ate together at a table in our backyard.

7. There were many delicious main dishes salads and desserts.

8. After that the children played games and the adults sat and talked.

9. In the evening we said our good-byes and everyone went home.

10. Then we washed and dried all the dishes.

PRACTICE 7.8

Writing Sentences with Commas

Take a piece of paper. Write answers to the questions. Use commas and the words in parentheses.

Examples: What are three things you do not own? (*or*)
I do not own a motorcycle, a horse, or a boat.

When were you born? (month/day/year)
I was born on January 1, 1988.

1. What are three foods you like? (*and*)

2. What are three foods you do not eat? (*or*)

3. What are three places you want to visit? (*and*)

4. What are three things you do in the morning? (*In the morning*)

5. What are two things you do on weekends? (*On weekends*)

6. What is today's date? (month/day/year)

7. When was your mother born? (month/day/year)

8. When was your father born? (month/day/year)

PART 3 | Grammar and Vocabulary

The Simple Past

Verbs in the **simple past** tense describe events that began and ended in the past.

Present	Past
I **watch** the news on TV every day.	I **watched** the news on TV yesterday.
Mr. Lee **is** a grandfather now.	Mr. Lee **was** a child in the 1950s.

The Simple Past: *Be*

Singular Subject	Be	
I	**was**	
You	**were**	
He		
She	**was**	here last week.
It		
My friend		

Plural Subject	Be	
We		
You		
They	**were**	here last week.
My friends		

Rules	Examples
1. Add *not* after *was* or *were* to make the statement negative.	I **was not** here last week. They **were not** there a month ago.
2. The past of *there is/are* is *there was/were*.	**There was** a meeting yesterday. **There were** no cars 200 years ago.
3. A past time expression can go at the beginning or end of a sentence.	I was at home **yesterday morning**. We were there **two weeks ago**. **In 1999**, Jack was in Brazil.

See page 168 for more information about past time expressions.

PRACTICE 7.9

Was/Were:
Affirmative
Statements

Change the sentences to the past. Use *was* or *were*.

1. I am here.

   Last Friday, __I was here.__

2. The train is on time.

   Yesterday, _____

3. You are my partner.

   _____ three days ago.

4. There are six people in the car.

   _____ last night.

5. My family is on vacation.

   Last August, _____

PRACTICE 7.10

Was/Were:
Negative
Statements

Change the sentences to the past. Use *was* or *were* + *not*. (Do not use *never*.)

1. I am never late for class.

   __I was not late for class_____ this morning.

2. You are never late for class.

   _____ yesterday.

3. You and I are never partners.

Last semester, _____

4. There are not four people in our group.

_____ a week ago.

5. There is never much rain here.

_____ last year.

6. My family is not here.

In 1998, _____

PRACTICE 7.11

Using Was/Were

Take a piece of paper. Answer the questions in complete sentences. Use *was* or *were*.

1. Where were you at 6:00 P.M. yesterday?

2. How was the weather yesterday?

3. When you were a child, who were your best friends?

4. When you were a child, what were your favorite stories or TV shows?

5. What color was your first (bicycle / car)?

6. Where were you in 2004?

7. Where were you in 1994?

8. Who were two important people in the history of your country?

The Simple Past: Regular Verbs

In simple past tense affirmative statements, **regular verbs** all end in *-ed*. Also, regular verbs are the same for all subjects.

Affirmative Statements

Subject	Simple Past Verb	
I	**washed**	my car yesterday.
She	**studied**	for the last test.
The rain	**stopped**	last night.
My parents	**arrived**	on Sunday.

See Appendix G for spelling rules for regular verbs in the simple past.

Negative Statements

Subject	*Did Not*	Base Form of Verb	
I		**wash**	my car last week.
She		**study**	for the first test.
The rain	**did not**	**stop**	before midnight.
My parents		**arrive**	on Saturday.

PRACTICE 7.12

Spelling Practice: Regular Verbs

Write the simple past tense form of each verb. Check Appendix G for spelling rules.

1. listen   _____listened_____   6. plan   _____

2. smile   _____   7. carry   _____

3. need   _____   8. decide   _____

4. stay   _____   9. ask   _____

5. cry   _____   10. fix   _____

PRACTICE 7.13

Regular Verbs: Negative Statements

Complete the sentences. Repeat the same verb, but make it negative. Use the past time expression in parentheses.

1. (last night) I often watch TV at night, but I __did not watch TV__

last night. _____

2. (last year) They often visit us, but they _____

_____

3. (yesterday) She often calls me, but she _____

_____

4. (last night) It often rains, but it _____

_____

5. (last weekend) He often washes his car, but he _____

_____

6. (last month) We often travel, but we _____

_____

PRACTICE 7.14

Using Regular Verbs in the Simple Past

Take a piece of paper. Write ten true statements using the simple past. Use verbs from the box. Include both affirmative and negative statements.

clean	fix	play	snow	study	wait
cook	listen	rain	stay	talk	walk

Examples: I listened to music on the radio last night.

It did not rain yesterday.

The Simple Past: Irregular Verbs

Irregular verbs do not end in *-ed* in the simple past.

Present	Past
I **go** to work every day.	I **went** to work yesterday.
She **does** her homework at night.	She **did** her homework last night.

Many common verbs are irregular. You must study them and memorize their simple past forms.

See Appendix H for a list of common irregular verbs and their simple past forms.

In negative statements, irregular verbs are like regular verbs. Use *did not* + the base form of the verb.

	Affirmative Statements	**Negative Statements**
Regular verb: *start*	We started work on time.	We **did not start** late.
Irregular verb: *begin*	We began work on time.	We **did not begin** late.

See Appendix G for contractions and questions in the simple past.

PRACTICE 7.15

Irregular Verbs: Affirmative Statements

Complete the sentences with the words given. Use the simple past.

1. I / take / a trip with my family

   In 1998, __I took a trip with my family.__

2. he / go / to his grandparents' house

   Last summer, _____

3. my cousins / come / to visit me

   _____ last year.

4. she / make / an important decision

   Two years ago, _____

5. they / leave / early

   _____ yesterday morning.

6. the children / have / fun

   _____ last weekend.

7. I / get / home at 8:00 P.M.

   _____ yesterday evening.

8. we / buy / new phones

   Last year, _____

PRACTICE 7.16

*Irregular Verbs:
Negative
Statements*

Change each statement from affirmative to negative.

1. We began our trip.   <u>We did not begin our trip.</u>

2. She came with us. _____

3. We had a good time. _____

4. You made a mistake. _____

5. He said good-bye. _____

6. She got upset. _____

7. I went home. _____

8. They did the right thing. _____

PRACTICE 7.17

*Reading and
Writing About
the Past*

Read the following story. Then answer the questions. Write complete sentences.

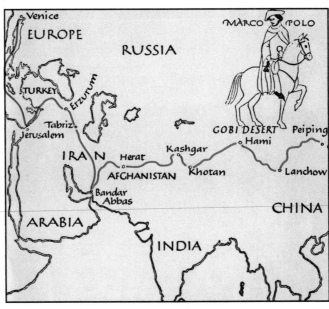

Marco Polo's route to Beijing

Marco Polo was a great traveler. He was born in Venice in 1254. At age seventeen, he left Venice with his father and his uncle. They began a 5,600-mile trip across Asia. It took them three and a half years, but they finally reached Beijing. Beijing was the capital city of

Kublai Khan, the powerful ruler of Mongolia and China. He liked Marco Polo and gave him work to do. Polo spent seventeen years in China, and he got rich there. He finally made the long trip back to Venice in 1295. Later, he wrote the story of his travels. His book was a great success in Europe. Polo died in 1324, but Europeans continued to read his book. In fact, for almost 600 years, they depended on his book for information about China.

1. Who was Marco Polo?

   He was a great traveler.

2. When was he born?

   _____

3. Where was he born?

   _____

4. Where did he go on his 5,600-mile trip?

   _____

5. How long did the trip take?

   _____

6. Who was Kublai Khan?

   _____

7. How long did Marco Polo stay in China?

   _____

8. What did Marco Polo do after his return to Europe?

   _____

PRACTICE 7.18

Editing: The Simple Past

Work alone or with a partner. Find and correct the twelve errors in verbs in this paragraph. The first error has been corrected for you.

                                   had
Last Monday, Harry ~~was have~~ a terrible day. The day begun badly. He did no hear his alarm clock, so he got up late. He did not has time for breakfast. He boughts coffee on the way to work and spilled it on his clothes. At work, he wrote reports all morning. At noon, his boss came in. He was angry. "You did not a good job on this report," he say to Harry. Harry felt bad. He no went out to lunch with his friends. Instead, he was stayed in his office and work. Finally, he finished. On the way home, he has a car accident. Poor Harry! At home, he goed back to bed. He wanted to forget the whole day.

PART 4 | The Writing Process

Your Paragraph: *An Important Day*

You are going to write a paragraph about a day that you remember well, like the model paragraphs on page 138.

Step 1: Prewrite

a. Get ready to write by doing a prewriting activity. Choose one of these activities:
- Make notes in time order about what happened on that day. (See page 141 for an example of notes in time order.)
- Freewrite about that day for at least five minutes. (See pages 141—142 for an explanation of freewriting and an example.)

Writer's Tip

Some writers like to do freewriting this way: First, they freewrite for five minutes. Next, they read what they wrote and choose one idea from their writing. Then they freewrite about that idea for five minutes more.

b. Work with a partner. Take turns describing your days. Then tell your partner three things you remember about his or her day.

c. Look at your notes or freewriting. Decide what information is most important to your description of the day. Circle or underline it. Decide how you want to organize your paragraph. Use time order, like model paragraph 1, or listing order, like model paragraph 2 (page 138).

 **Step 2: Write**

Write your first draft. Begin with a topic sentence. See the models on page 138 for examples. Make sure your supporting sentences show why your topic sentence is true.

 **Step 3: Edit**

a. Read your paragraph again. It may help you to read it out loud. Make changes if needed.

b. Edit your paper carefully. Check for mistakes before you show it to anyone.

c. Peer review: Exchange papers with a partner. Follow the Reviewer's Checklist on page 158. Check (✓) each box when you finish that step.

Reviewer's Checklist — Chapter 7

Your partner's name: _____

<u>Content</u>

☐ Read all of your partner's paragraph.

☐ Underline any part of the paragraph you do not understand. Ask your partner to explain it.

☐ Circle the topic sentence. Write *TS* on the paper if there is no topic sentence.

☐ Reread the supporting sentences. Ask questions if you want more information.

<u>Form</u>

Look at these parts of your partner's paper. Mark any problems on the paper in pencil. Put a question mark (?) if you are not sure about something.

☐ the format of the paper ☐ the use of simple past verbs

☐ a subject in every sentence ☐ the use of commas

☐ a verb for every subject

---

d. Return your partner's paper. Say something nice about the paragraph.

e. Look at your own paper. If you do not agree with a comment, ask another student or your teacher.

Step 4: Write the Final Draft

a. On your first draft, mark any changes you want to make. Then take another piece of paper and write a new draft.

b. Edit your new draft carefully, and hand it in to your teacher.

Results of the Writing Process

Your teacher will give you feedback on your paragraph. Look carefully at your teacher's comments and marks on the paper. Ask your teacher about anything you do not understand. Your teacher may ask you to write a new draft.

Check your new draft carefully before you hand it in. Remember to hand in your old and new drafts together, with the new draft on top.

When you do not need to rewrite your paragraph, save it in your folder.

Expansion Activities

Your Journal

Continue making entries in your journal. If you cannot think of a topic for a journal entry, try one of these ideas:

- How was this past weekend? Did you have fun? Did you do anything special, or was it just a typical weekend? Describe what you did.
- Write about your education. How old were you when you started school? What schools did you go to? How did you feel about school?
- Think of a time when you had some good luck. What happened? Why do you think you were lucky?
- Think of someone who was important to you when you were growing up. Who was this person? Why was he or she important in your life?
- When did you start learning English? Did you choose to study English, or did you have to learn it? Describe your first experiences with learning English.

Challenge: *A Funny or Scary Experience*

Write a paragraph about a funny or scary experience. First, choose a prewriting activity: brainstorming and taking notes (see page 132), listing notes in time order (see page 141), or freewriting (see page 142). Write a lot of ideas before you start your first draft.

Begin your paragraph with a topic sentence. In your topic sentence, tell the reader what kind of experience you are going to describe. Be sure to include enough details in your paragraph.

Ask a friend or a classmate to review your first draft. Use the Reviewer's Checklist on page 158. Then prepare a final draft and give it to your teacher.

Memories of a Trip

Going on a trip!

Chapter Preview

Work with a partner or in a small group. Read the model paragraphs. Answer the questions that follow.

MODEL

Paragraph 1

A Trip with My Family

I have a happy memory from my childhood. When I was small, my family took a trip to a lake. It was in the summer. We went there early in the morning and stayed all day. I remember playing games on the grass with my brothers and sisters. We had fun climbing trees, too. At noon, my father built a fire, and we made shish kebab. It was delicious. After that, I remember listening to my sister tell stories. I did not want to leave when it was time to go home. I had a lot of fun that day, so I like to remember our trip to the lake.

MODEL

Paragraph 2

The Trip That Changed My Life

My trip to the United States was a big shock. One day, my mother said, "Go and pack your clothes. Tomorrow we are going to live in New York." The news was a complete surprise to me. I went to my room and sat on the bed for a long time. Then I called my best friend. The next morning, my mother and I got on a plane. I remember sitting next to the window and looking down on my city. I remember feeling scared about my future. After we landed in New York, my aunt picked us up, and we went to stay with her. My life changed overnight. I will never forget that trip.

Questions about model paragraph 1:

1. The writer uses the first two sentences to introduce the topic and the controlling idea.

   a. What is the topic? _____

   b. What does the writer say about it? _____

2. What details does the writer give about the trip?

   a. When did it happen? _____

   b. What did the writer do? _____

   _____

3. Did the writer use time order to organize the paragraph? (Yes / No)

4. Complete these sentences with the words the writer used.

   a. I _____ games on the grass with my
      brothers and sisters.

   b. After that, I _____ to my sister tell
      stories.

Questions about model paragraph 2:

1. What is the topic sentence? Copy it below. Circle the topic and
   underline the controlling idea.

   _____

2. Why was the trip a shock for the writer? Check (✓) your answers.

   ☐ His mother's plans surprised him.

   ☐ He had to say good-bye to his mother.

   ☐ He was afraid to get on an airplane.

   ☐ Big changes happened in his life very fast.

3. Did the writer use time order to organize the paragraph? (Yes / No)

4. Complete these sentences with the words the writer used.

   a. I _____ next to the window and looking
      down on my city.

   b. I _____ scared about my future.

5. Complete these sentences with the verbs the writer used.

a. One day, my mother _____, "Go and pack your clothes."

b. After we _____ in New York, my aunt _____ us up, and we _____ to stay with her.

c. My life _____ overnight.

What tense are the verbs you wrote in 5a–c? _____

You will write a paragraph about a trip that you took later in this chapter (page 175).

PART 1 | Organization

Concluding Sentences

Some paragraphs end with a **concluding sentence**. *Concluding* means "finishing" or "completing." A concluding sentence marks the end of the writer's comments on the topic. It usually connects to information in the topic sentence. Below are two ways for a concluding sentence to do that.

(1) Sometimes a concluding sentence repeats words from the topic sentence, to bring the reader back to the main idea:

TOPIC SENTENCE

When I take a trip, I prefer to go by train. The seats on trains are very comfortable. They give me enough space for my legs. I like the big windows on trains, too. I enjoy looking out at the views, especially in the country. I also like being free to leave my seat. I can stand up and walk around on a train when I want to.

CONCLUDING SENTENCE

These are just a few of the reasons why I like traveling by train.

(2) Sometimes the writer ends the paragraph with a personal comment about the topic:

TOPIC

Meriwether Lewis and William Clark were important American explorers. In 1803, President Thomas Jefferson asked them to find out about a new part of the United States. For almost three years, they explored from Missouri to the Pacific Ocean and back, a trip of 8,000 miles. A young Native American woman named Sacagawea helped them find their way. It was a difficult and dangerous trip, but they brought back a great deal of valuable information about the area.

PERSONAL COMMENT

I admire Lewis and Clark because they were brave, smart, and adventurous.

PRACTICE 8.1

Making Connections

Underline the topic sentence and the concluding sentence. Circle the words that connect them.

Last spring, I had fun on a camping trip. I went with friends from my high school in Puerto Rico. First, we took a bus from our hometown, San Juan, to the town of Fajardo. Then we took a boat from Fajardo to the island of Culebra. There is a beautiful beach there called Playa Flamenco. We camped near the beach for five days. I got a sunburn and many insect bites, but I did not care. I had a great time camping with my friends.

Read each paragraph. Then choose the best concluding sentence. Write that sentence on the lines.

1.
The Secrets to a Successful Restaurant

There are four keys to running a successful restaurant. First, the food must taste good. Boring or bad food will not bring in customers. Second, the dining room must be a comfortable and attractive place. People should feel good spending time in the restaurant. Third, there must be good service. Both the kitchen staff and the servers need to do their jobs well. Finally, the price must be right. There must be a good match between the cost and the dining experience. _____
_____

a. The restaurant should stay open late, too.
b. Many new restaurants have to close after just a few months.
c. A restaurant that does well in these four areas will be a success.

2.
A Wonderful City

There are three main reasons why I love Florence, Italy. First of all, I enjoy the people of Florence. They are friendly, interesting, and good-looking. Second, I like to hear people speak Italian. I think it is a beautiful language. Finally, I love the food in Florence. You can get delicious things to eat in the markets, shops, and restaurants.

a. Millions of people visit Florence because it is an important city.
b. The people, language, and food make Florence one of my favorite places.
c. It is also very interesting to learn about the art and history of this beautiful city.

3.

The Power of Television

Television has a big influence on children today. In some countries, children spend a lot of time watching it. For example, in the United States, the average child watches television three or four hours a day. Many children spend more time each year in front of a TV than in school. _____

_____

 a. As a result, television can influence how children think and act.
 b. In addition, the Internet has a very strong effect on many children.
 c. In fact, almost all American homes today have one or more TV sets.

4.

An Easy Recipe

Peanut butter cookies are very easy to make. The following recipe has only four ingredients and takes only a few minutes. Start by beating an egg in a mixing bowl. Add one cup of sugar, one cup of peanut butter, and one teaspoon of vanilla. Mix everything well. Using a spoon, drop small amounts of dough onto a cookie sheet. Bake the cookies for 10 minutes at 325°F. _____

 a. Chocolate chip cookies need a little more work.
 b. I hope you will like these cookies as much as I do.
 c. Peanut butter sandwiches are very easy to make, too.

5.

Getting Drinking Water from the Ocean

One way to get drinking water is to take the salt out of ocean water. The process of taking the salt out is called *desalination*. Many countries use this process to get drinking water. Most of them are in the Middle East, the Caribbean, and the Mediterranean. They need the water for homes, farms, and businesses. However, there is a problem with desalination. It is very expensive. For that reason, only one percent (1%) of the world's drinking water now comes from the ocean. We need to learn how to make the process less expensive. _____

 a. Of course, people need clean water.
 b. In addition, water power can give us clean energy.
 c. Then we can get more drinking water from the ocean.

PART 2 | Grammar and Vocabulary

Past Time Expressions

A past time expression tells when something happened. In Chapter 7, you learned that it usually comes at the beginning or end of a sentence.

I went to the movies **yesterday**.

Yesterday, I went to the movies.

Using *Ago* or *Last*

Rules	Examples
1. Use an amount of time + *ago*.	It happened **many years ago**. They left **five minutes ago**.
2. Use *last* + a period of time.	It happened **last summer**. They left **last week**.

PRACTICE 8.3

Past Time Expressions

Write *ago* or *last*.

(1)__Last__ year, Raquel took several business trips. In January, she was in South Africa for ten days. Then she went to Brazil (2) _____ March. It was not her first trip to South America. She was also there in 2000 and again four years (3) _____. Her next trip was (4) _____ May, to Hong Kong. She has been there several times, too. In fact, she was there again a week (5) _____. Then (6) _____ fall, Raquel went on two trips to Europe. Many years (7) _____, when she was a little girl, she dreamed about seeing the world. Now her dream has come true.

Prepositional Phrases for Describing Past Time

Rules	Examples
1. Use *in* + a month, season, or year.	It happened **in July**. It happened **in 1922**.
2. Use *on* + a specific day or date.	It happened **on July 1**, 1922. The baby was born **on Friday**.
3. Use *for* + an amount of time.	We waited **for fifteen minutes**.

See pages 88 and 128–130 for more information about prepositional phrases.

PRACTICE 8.4

Prepositions for Describing Past Time

Write *in, on,* or *for*.

1. He graduated _in_ 2006.
2. I was born _in_ March 13, 1987.
3. We stayed there _for_ ten days.
4. I bought my ticket _on_ Monday.
5. She went on vacation _in_ April.
6. They were away _for_ a week.
7. They left _in_ August.
8. Their trip began _on_ August 8.
9. We waited _for_ an hour.
10. We got married _in_ the spring.
11. The wedding was _on_ May 1, 2001.
12. Our son was born _in_ 2003.

PRACTICE 8.5

Writing About Past Time

Take a piece of paper. Write eight true statements about your life. Use the time expressions given.

Example: yesterday
I went to my classes yesterday.

1. yesterday
2. last weekend
3. last summer
4. one year ago
5. in 1999
6. for a long time
7. for _____ years
8. _____ years ago

Before and *After* as Prepositions

Before and *after* are prepositions. Prepositional phrases with *before* or *after* + a noun describe time.

Rules	Examples
1. Use *after* + an earlier event.	They took a trip **after** <u>their wedding</u>. (first, the wedding; then the trip)
2. Use *before* + a later event.	I talked to the teacher **before** <u>class</u>. (first, the talk; then the class)
3. Put the phrase at the beginning or end of a sentence. The meaning is the same.	**Before** <u>class</u>, I talked to the teacher. (first, the talk; then the class)
4. Put a comma after a prepositional phrase at the beginning of a sentence.	**After their wedding**, they took a trip.

PRACTICE 8.6

Before and After: Combining Sentences

Work alone or with a partner. Combine the two sentences, keeping the time and word order the same. Use *after* or *before* + the **boldfaced** words.

Examples: after
~~We finished~~ **work**. We went fishing.
After work, we went fishing.

before
I washed my hands. ~~I had~~ **lunch**.
I washed my hands before lunch.

1. I studied. I took **the test**.

   _____

2. He had **an interview**. He got the job.

   _____

3. I spent **a day at the beach**. I had a sunburn.

   _____

4. I sent out invitations. I had **my birthday party**.

   _____

5. We went on **our vacation**. We told our friends about it.

_____

6. He read the newspaper. He went to **work**.

_____

PRACTICE 8.7

Using Before _and_ After + _a_ _Noun_

Take a piece of paper. Write four true statements with _before_ + a noun and four true statements with _after_ + a noun. Use the nouns in the box, or choose other nouns.

Examples: People often feel nervous before an exam.

I had coffee after my first class.

| breakfast | class | dinner | exam | lunch | party |

PART 3 | Sentence Structure

Sentences with Past Time Clauses

Past Time Clauses and Main Clauses

A **past time clause** tells when something happened.

They saw the Taj Mahal. When did they see it?

They saw the Taj Mahal **when they were in India**.

A past time clause must have three things: a time word, a subject, and a verb.

We said good-bye **before** **we** **left**.

A past time clause is never a complete sentence by itself. It must connect to a **main clause**. A main clause can be a complete sentence.

I went to Buenos Aires. = a complete sentence

MAIN CLAUSE   PAST TIME CLAUSE
I went to Buenos Aires **after I finished school**.

Sentences with time clauses are **complex sentences**. See Appendix K for more information.

PRACTICE 8.8

Recognizing Main and Past Time Clauses

Work alone or with a partner. Look at each group of words below. Check (✓) **Main Clause** or **Past Time Clause**.

Main Clause	Past Time Clause	
☐	☑	1. when Mei Li and I heard about the concert
☑	☐	2. we decided to buy tickets
☐	☐	3. we stood in line for an hour before the concert
☐	☐	4. a lot of our friends came
☐	☐	5. before the concert started
☐	☐	6. the concert lasted more than three hours
☐	☐	7. the band played some of their greatest hits
☐	☐	8. after they played some of their new music
☐	☐	9. when the concert ended
☐	☐	10. Mei Li and I went out to eat

Past Time Clauses with *Before, After,* and *When*

Before, after, and *when* are **subordinating conjunctions** in time clauses.

Rules	Examples
1. Use *after* + something that happened earlier.	THIS HAPPENED **FIRST.** He went to bed **after** <u>he brushed his teeth.</u>
2. Use *before* + something that happened later.	THIS HAPPENED **LATER.** He brushed his teeth **before** <u>he went to bed.</u>
3. Use *when* + something that happened at the same time or soon afterward.	THIS HAPPENED **AT THE SAME TIME.** Everybody cried **when** <u>we said good-bye.</u>
4. A past time clause can come before or after the main clause. Put a comma after the time clause when it comes first.	**When we said good-bye,** everybody cried.

Do not put a comma after the word *after*. Do not put *after* at the end of a sentence.

after + subject + verb	**After we met** for coffee, we went to class.
after + noun	**After coffee,** we went to class.
After that,	We met for coffee. **After that,** we went to class.

PRACTICE 8.9

Complex Sentences with Before and After

Work alone or with a partner. Write *1* above the action that happened first and *2* above the action that happened later. Underline the past time clause.

1. Mariela and Ricardo met <u>after they entered the London School of Economics.</u>

2. Mariela knew Ricardo's friends before she met him.

3. After Ricardo heard about Mariela, he wanted to meet her.

4. He fell in love soon after he met her.

5. Before Mariela agreed to marry him, Ricardo had to meet her family in Venezuela.

6. Ricardo and Mariela graduated from the university before they got married.

7. They went on a honeymoon after they got married.

8. After they returned from their trip, they found jobs in Caracas.

PRACTICE 8.10

Using Past Time Clauses

Take a piece of paper. Write sentences with past time clauses to answer the questions. Use *after, before,* and *when.* Underline each past time clause.

Examples: When did you start school?
I started school <u>when I was five years old</u>.

When did you buy a ticket before you did something?
I bought a ticket <u>before I took a train last weekend</u>.

1. Did your parents decide on your name before or after you were born?

2. When did you start learning English?

3. Did you get this book before or after you went to the first class?

4. When did you buy new clothes before you did something?

5. When did you feel nervous before you did something?

6. When did you feel good after you did something?

7. When did you make an important decision?

8. When did you have fun with a friend?

Sentence Fragments

A fragment is a broken piece of something. A **sentence fragment** is a piece of a sentence, not a complete sentence. Something is missing.

A past time clause by itself is a sentence fragment.

FRAGMENT   COMPLETE SENTENCE
<u>After Noriko arrived</u>. We made popcorn.

Here are two ways to correct a fragment like *After Noriko arrived.*

(1) Connect the fragment to a complete sentence.

After Noriko arrived, we made popcorn.

We made popcorn **after Noriko arrived.**

(2) Change the fragment to make it a complete sentence.

At 8:00 P.M., Noriko arrived.

PRACTICE 8.11

Editing:
Sentence
Fragments

Work alone or with a partner. Read the paragraph. Correct the five sentence fragments. Add commas as needed. The first fragment has been corrected for you.

Yesterday, Vincent went ~~shopping. After~~ *shopping after* he finished his classes. He needed new running shoes because his old shoes were worn out. After he arrived at the store. He started trying on shoes. Some shoes did not feel right, and some were too expensive. He tried on several pairs of shoes. Before he found the right ones. When he went to pay for them. He realized that he did not have his wallet. It was not in his pocket. He asked the salesclerk to hold the shoes for him. He needed to come back later. After he found his wallet in his room. He went back and got his new shoes.

PART 4 | The Writing Process

A. Your Paragraph: *Memories of a Trip*

You are going to write a paragraph about a trip you took, like the model paragraphs on page 162.

Step 1: Prewrite

a. Get ready to write by doing a prewriting activity. Choose one of the following activities:

- Make notes about the trip in time order. (See page 141 for an example of notes in time order.)
- Freewrite about the trip for at least five minutes. (See pages 141—142 for an explanation of freewriting and an example.)

b. Find a partner and take turns asking about each other's trip. Ask questions like the following:

Where did you go on your trip?

When did you go?

Who went with you?

How long was your trip?

What did you do on your trip?

How did you feel about the trip?

c. Look again at your notes or freewriting. Add notes as needed. Include answers to the questions above. Underline the information that will be most important to describe your trip.

Step 2: Write

Write your first draft. Begin your paragraph with a topic sentence. See the models on page 162 for examples. Give details in your supporting sentences. End your paragraph with a concluding sentence. Try to include both past time expressions and past time clauses.

Step 3: Edit

a. Read your paragraph again. It may help you to read it out loud. Make changes if needed.

b. Edit your paper carefully. Check for mistakes before you show it to anyone.

c. Peer review: Exchange papers with a partner. Follow the Reviewer's Checklist on page 177. Check (✓) each box when you finish that step.

d. Return your partner's paper. Say something nice about the paragraph.

e. Look at your own paper. If you do not agree with a comment, then ask another student or your teacher.

Reviewer's Checklist — Chapter 8

Your partner's name: _____

Content

☐ Read all of your partner's paragraph.

☐ Underline any part of the paragraph you do not understand. Ask your partner to explain it.

☐ Circle the topic sentence. Write *TS* on the paper if there is no topic sentence.

☐ Reread the supporting sentences. Ask questions if you want more information.

☐ Circle the concluding sentence. Write *CS* on the paper if there is no concluding sentence.

Form

Look at these parts of your partner's paper. Mark any problems on the paper in pencil. Put a question mark (?) if you are not sure about something.

☐ the format of the paper   ☐ the use of past tense verbs

☐ a subject in every sentence   ☐ the use of *before* and *after*

☐ a verb for every subject   ☐ the use of commas

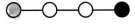

Step 4: Write the Final Draft

a. On your first draft, mark any changes you want to make. Then take another piece of paper and write a new draft.

b. Edit your new draft carefully. Then hand it in to your teacher.

Results of the Writing Process

Your teacher may ask you to write another draft after he or she reads your paper. Check your new draft carefully before you hand it in. Remember to hand in your old and new drafts together, with the new draft on top.

When you do not need to rewrite a paragraph, put it in your folder.

Expansion Activities

Your Journal

Continue making entries in your journal. If you cannot think of a topic for a journal entry, try one of these ideas:

- Write about another trip you remember. Tell where and when you made this trip. Focus on describing one thing that you heard, smelled, saw, or tasted on this trip.
- Describe a time when someone or something surprised you. What happened? Was it a good or a bad surprise? Why?
- Write about an important decision you made. What did you decide? Why did you make this decision? Do you think your decision was good or bad?
- Write a short biography of one of your parents, one of your grandparents, or another older person. (*Biography* means "the story of a person's life.")
- Write about one of your earliest memories of English. Did you hear a song in English? Did you learn a word in English? Why do you remember this event?

Challenge: *From My Childhood*

Write a paragraph about one of your favorite possessions from when you were a child. It could be a favorite toy, a pet, or a piece of clothing, for example. First, choose a prewriting activity: brainstorming and taking notes (see page 132), making notes in time order (see page 141), or freewriting (see page 142).

Write a first draft. Begin your paragraph with a topic sentence. Be sure to include enough details to support your main idea. End your paragraph with a concluding sentence.

Ask a friend or a classmate to review your first draft. Use the Reviewer's Checklist on page 177. Then prepare a final draft and give it to your teacher.

Looking Ahead

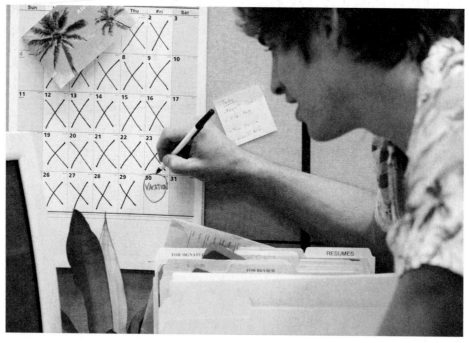

I can't wait!

Chapter Preview

Chapter Preview

Work with a partner or in a small group. Read the model paragraphs. Answer the questions that follow.

MODEL

Paragraph 1

Planning for My Son's Birthday

I am looking forward to my son's birthday. In two weeks, he is going to be four years old, and we are going to have a party for him at home. We are going to invite about ten or twelve friends and relatives to the party. First, the children will play, and the adults will talk. Then we will have lunch. My wife is going to make a birthday cake for the party. After we have the cake, my son will open his presents. I am going to give him a remote-control car because he asked for that. I hope he will like it, and I hope his birthday will be happy.

MODEL

Paragraph 2

My Future

I have big plans for my future. I am going to study nursing after I learn more English. I am going to finish the English program here before I transfer to a university. At the university, I plan to get a bachelor's degree in nursing. After I become a nurse, I am going to work in a hospital. I hope that I will find a good job. I am also planning to get married someday. I hope that I will meet a kind and intelligent man. I would like to have four children, two boys and two girls. I am looking forward to my career, but my family will be the most important part of my future.

Questions about model paragraph 1:

1. What is the topic of this paragraph? _____

2. What does "I am looking forward to" mean? Circle your answer.

    a. I am nervous about (something in the future).

    b. I am excited about (something in the future).

3. Complete these sentences about the paragraph.

    a. The writer hopes that his son _____

    b. He also hopes _____

4. Does the writer use time order to organize his paragraph? Circle: (Yes / No)

5. Complete these sentences with the verbs the writer uses to describe future events.

    a. In two weeks, he _____ four years old, and we

    _____ a party for him at home.

    b. First, the children _____, and the adults

    _____

Questions about model paragraph 2:

1. What is the topic sentence? Copy it here. _____

    _____

2. Put the writer's goals in the order she expects to reach them. Number them from 1 to 6.

    ☐ have children   ☐ get a job in a hospital

    ☐ learn more English   ☐ get a bachelor's degree

    ☐ study nursing   ☐ transfer to a university

3. What word means "at some time far in the future"?

    _____

4. What word means "many years of work in a professional job"?

    _____

5. Complete these sentences from the paragraph. Write the **future time clauses**.

   a. I am going to study nursing _____

   b. I am going to finish the English program here _____

   _____

   c. _____ I am going to work in a hospital.

6. Circle the verb in each future time clause that you wrote above (5a, b, c). Which tense are the three verbs you wrote? (simple present / future)

Later in this chapter (page 196), you will write a paragraph about something you look forward to in your future.

PART 1 | Organization

Listing Order and Listing-Order Words

One way to organize a paragraph about the future is to use time order. The writers of both model paragraphs on page 181 used time order.

Another way to organize a paragraph about the future is to use listing order. A writer can use listing order if he or she does not know the time order of future events.

Read this paragraph by the writer of model paragraph 2 on page 181. She is writing about the same future plans, but here she uses listing order. Her topic sentence tells us that the paragraph will list her three goals.

I have three major goals for my future. **First**, I want a good education. I am going to learn more English and go to a university. I plan to get a bachelor's degree in nursing. I **also** want to get married and have a family. I hope that I will meet a kind and intelligent man someday, a man who loves children. I would like to have four children, two boys and two girls. **Finally**, I want to have a good career as a nurse. I am going to do my best to reach these three goals.

The three **boldfaced** words in the paragraph on page 183 are **listing-order words**. They introduce each of the writer's three goals. Notice the position of *also* in *I also want to get married*. All the other listing-order words go at the beginning of the sentence.

Here are some more listing-order words and phrases:

First of all,	Second,	Third,	also	In addition,

For more examples of paragraphs with listing order, see the following:

- "My Wedding Day" on page 138
- "The Secrets to a Successful Restaurant" on page 166
- "A Wonderful City" on page 166

When you read these paragraphs, notice the topic sentences and the listing-order words and phrases.

PRACTICE 9.1

Listing-Order Paragraphs: Topic Sentences

Work alone or with a partner. Check (✓) the topic sentences that tell the reader the paragraph will be in listing order.

☑ 1. There are three reasons why I want to be a lawyer.

☐ 2. There are several different kinds of engineers.

☐ 3. Becoming a doctor will take me a long time.

☐ 4. A good nurse must have four important qualities.

☐ 5. My grandfather had an important career in public service.

☐ 6. I have two main reasons for wanting to be a teacher.

☐ 7. My mother changed careers at age forty.

☐ 8. The Career Development Office can help students in several ways.

PRACTICE 9.2
Listing-Order Words

Circle the correct listing-order words for this paragraph.

I plan to accomplish four things this weekend. (1. Also / First), I am going to play tennis with my brother, and I am going to win. That is going to be great. I am (2. also / second) going to do something about the dirty clothes on the floor of my room. Maybe I will wash some of them. (3. Finally / In addition), I am going to fill out an application for a part-time job at the library. I think the application is on my floor somewhere. (4. Finally / First of all), I am going to work on a paper for my psychology class. It is due soon, so I really need to get started. Those are my goals for the weekend. Wish me luck!

PART 2 | Grammar and Vocabulary

Expressing Future Time with *Be Going To*

Verbs with *be going to* express future time.

Affirmative Statements with *Be Going To*

Singular			
Subject	*Be*	*Going To*	**Base Verb**
I	am		
You	are		
He		going to	win.
She			
It	is		
Tony			

Plural			
Subject	*Be*	*Going To*	**Base Verb**
We			
You			
They	are	going to	win.
The men			

See Appendix D for the contracted forms of am, is, *and* are (+ not).

Rules	Examples
1. Use *will* for predictions about the future. In this case, *will* and *be going to* have the same meaning.	You **will love** this song. = You are going to love this song.
2. To form the negative, add *not* after *will*.	The meeting **will not** take long.
3. Use *be going to*, usually not *will*, for plans you have already made.	are going to Chris and I ~~will~~ **get** married.

Writer's Tip

Use *and* to join two verbs. Do not repeat *will* or *be going to*.

She **will call and** ~~will~~ **tell him**.

She **is going to call and** ~~is going to~~ **tell him**.

PRACTICE 9.5

Making Predictions with Will

Rewrite these predictions. Use *will*. (*Note*: The meaning of the sentences does not change.)

Example: The flight is going to take about six hours.

    The flight will take about six hours.

1. I think you are going to enjoy your trip to Hawaii.

   _____

2. The weather is going to be great.

   _____

3. You are not going to need warm clothes.

   _____

Surfing

4. The surfing is going to be excellent.

_____

5. The beaches are not going to be crowded.

_____

6. We are going to miss you.

_____

PRACTICE 9.6

*Editing:
Statements
About the
Future*

Work alone or with a partner. Find and correct the verb error in each statement. (*Note*: There is more than one way to make the corrections.)

                           be

1. Dinner will ~~to be~~ ready soon. **or** *Dinner is going to be ready soon.*

2. It's will be sunny tomorrow.

3. I think my brothers going to study chemistry.

4. Your adviser will going to help you.

5. I think Brazil will winning the next World Cup.

6. Hiral is going have her baby in May.

7. The party going to start at 9:00 P.M.

8. Juan Carlos will goes to work at 3:00 P.M.

9. The next bus will coming soon.

10. I think I'm will need a ride tomorrow.

Future Time Expressions

Future time expressions tell when events will happen. They can help show the time and order of events in a paragraph.

Using *This*, *Next*, or *In*

Rules	Examples
1. Use *this* + a specific time period. The time period is happening now or will start soon.	I am going to leave **this evening**. They will finish the job **this week**.
2. Use *next* + a specific time period. The time period has not yet started.	I am going to leave **next Monday**. They will finish the job **next week**.
3. Use *in* + an amount of time (as in a number of hours, days, or years). The event will happen after that time passes.	He is going to be here **in a minute**. **In two weeks**, it will be spring.

PRACTICE 9.7

This, Next, *or* In

Circle the correct word.

1. Jack is going to graduate (in / this) two years.

2. This summer, I am going to take classes, but (this / next) summer, I am going to work.

3. Rima is studying this morning because she is going to have an exam (in / this) afternoon.

4. The students are on spring break now, so there are no classes (this / next) week.

5. Professor: Your papers are due on Tuesday.

   Students: Do you mean tomorrow?

   Professor: No, not this week. (Next / In) Tuesday.

6. The semester began three weeks ago. It will end (next / in) twelve weeks.

PRACTICE 9.8

Using Future Time Expressions

Take a piece of paper. Write complete sentences to answer the questions. Include the time expressions.

1. What are you going to do tomorrow?

2. Where are you going to be the day after tomorrow?

3. What are you going to do this weekend?

4. Where are you going to be next week?

5. What is going to happen in a few years?

PART 3 | Sentence Structure

Sentences with Future Time Clauses

Future Time Clauses and Main Clauses

A **future time clause** tells when something will happen.

I am going to study. When are you going to study?

I am going to study **before I go to bed**.

A future time clause must have three things: a time word, a subject, and a verb.

          1   2   3
I will call you **when I arrive.**

A future time clause is never a complete sentence by itself. It must connect to a main clause. A main clause can be a complete sentence.

He is going to get a job. = a complete sentence

After he graduates. = a sentence fragment

      MAIN CLAUSE   FUTURE TIME CLAUSE
He is going to get a job **after he graduates**.

Sentences with time clauses are **complex sentences**. See Appendix K for more information.

PRACTICE 9.9

Identifying Future Time Clauses

Work alone or with a partner. Check (✓) the sentences with future time clauses. Underline the future time clause. The first one has been done.

☐ 1. Vote for me next election day!

☑ 2. <u>When I become president,</u> I will work for world peace.

☐ 3. Together, we are going to put an end to all wars.

☐ 4. I am also going to make education a high priority.

☐ 5. After I am president, there will be more money for our children's schools.

☐ 6. I am going to make sure we have clean air and clean water.

☐ 7. I will stop polluters before they destroy our environment.

☐ 8. I am going to do great things after I win this election!

Future Time Clauses with *Before*, *After*, and *When*

The time words *before, after*, and *when* can introduce future time clauses.

Rules	Examples
1. Use a simple present verb in a future time clause. Do not use *will* or *be going to*.	The meeting will start **when everyone is here**. He will say good-bye **before he <u>leaves</u>**.
2. A future time clause can come before or after the main clause. The meaning is the same. Put a comma after a time clause when it comes first.	I am going to go to medical school **after I finish college**. **After I finish college**, I am going to go to medical school.
3. Remember, *before* and *after* can also be prepositions.	I am going to go to graduate school **after college**.

Before, after, and *when* are **subordinating conjunctions** in time clauses. See Appendix K for more information.

See page 170 for more information about *before* and *after* as prepositions.

PRACTICE 9.10

Sentences with Future Time Clauses: Verbs

Work alone or with a partner. Mark the main clause and the future time clause in each sentence. Circle the correct verb.

1. Sonia and Tony are going to get married after they ((finish) / will finish) school.

2. I (am / will be) there when they have their wedding in June.

3. After they (are / are going to be) married, they are going to take a trip.

4. When they (come / will come) back, they are going to find work.

5. They (look / will look) for a place to live after they have jobs.

6. They are going to wait a few years before they (have / will have) children.

7. Before they start a family, they (buy / are going to buy) a house.

8. I hope they will be very happy when they (are / will be) married.

PRACTICE 9.11

Using Future Time Clauses

Take a piece of paper. Copy and complete the following sentences.

1. After I finish this exercise, . . .

2. Before I go to bed tonight, . . .

3. . . . after I get up tomorrow.

4. I am going to have something to eat . . .

5. . . . , I am going to relax.

6. . . . , I will be happy.

Run-On Sentences

A **run-on sentence** is a mistake. Run-on sentences happen when writers do not connect sentences correctly. Look at these four examples and the ways to correct them.

1. **Run-On:**	My brother's name is Osman he is sixteen years old.
Problem:	There is no connecting word.
Correction:	Add a comma + *and*.
	My brother's name is Osman, and he is sixteen years old.
2. **Run-On:**	They are going to save their money, then they will buy a house.
Problem:	*Then* is not a connecting word.
Correction:	Separate the two simple sentences.
	They are going to save their money. Then they will buy a house.
3. **Run-On:**	I am going to study math, I want to become an engineer.
Problem:	A comma cannot connect two sentences.
Correction:	Connect the verbs with *and*.
	I am going to study math and become an engineer.
4. **Run-On:**	First, he will wash the clothes, after he will dry them.
Problem:	The word *after* is used incorrectly.
Correction:	(a) Write a compound sentence with *and then*.
	First, he will wash the clothes, and then he will dry them.
	(b) Use a future time clause with *after*.
	After he washes the clothes, he will dry them.

PRACTICE 9.12

Identifying Run-On Sentences

Work alone or with a partner. Write *RO* next to each run-on sentence. Write *OK* next to each correct sentence.

1. _OK_ In the year 2025, I think my life will be very different.

2. _RO_ I will be much older I will be middle-aged.

3. ____ I am not married now, in 2025 I think I will be married.

4. ____ I hope to get married in a few years, after, I hope we will have children.

5. ____ Now I do not own a house, but I hope to have a nice one in 2025.

6. ____ I am going to finish my education, then I will begin my career.

7. ____ After I begin my career, I am going to work very hard.

8. ____ I hope to have a good job in 2025, so my family can live well.

PRACTICE 9.13

Correcting Run-On Sentences

Work alone or with a partner. Correct these run-on sentences. There is more than one way to correct each sentence.

1. ~~We~~ When we said good-bye to our friends, I felt sad about leaving my homeland.

2. We began our trip it was very cold.

3. We arrived at the airport, then we went to the ticket counter and checked our bags.

4. This was my first time on a plane it felt like a bus at first.

5. The plane left the ground, it made my stomach feel strange.

6. We flew for a few hours, after we landed in Canada.

7. We walked off the plane my relatives were there.

8. I missed my friends, I was excited about starting a new life.

PRACTICE 9.14

Editing: Run-On Sentences

Work alone or with a partner. Find and correct the seven run-on sentences in this paragraph. The first run-on sentence has been corrected for you. There is more than one way to make a correction.

Someday, I am going to take a trip around the world. I plan to spend six months on my trip, and I expect to travel mostly by plane. My first stop will be in Hawaii I want to try surfing and visit a

Pyramids in Egypt

volcano. From Hawaii, I am going to fly to Japan, I also want to visit Korea, China, Taiwan, Thailand, and Indonesia. In each country, I am going to spend some time in cities, I especially want to see Kyoto and Beijing. I also hope to visit the countryside. After two months in Asia, I am going to fly to eastern Africa. I want to go on a photo safari to see wild animals, of course, I will have my camera. My next flight will take me north to Egypt, so I can see the pyramids, after that, I am going to travel to Istanbul. I look forward to spending the last part of my trip in the great cities of Europe, cities like Athens, Rome, Berlin, and St. Petersburg. I am going to need a lot of money for this trip, I think I am going to need more than six months, too!

PART 4 | The Writing Process

Your Paragraph: *My Future Plans*

You are going to write a paragraph about something that you are looking forward to in your future. You can write about something that you are planning to do soon, or you can write about your long-term plans. Remember to use *be going to* when you write about plans.

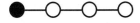

Step 1: Prewrite

a. Get ready to write by doing some prewriting. Choose one of these activities:

- Make notes in time order about what is going to happen. (See page 141 for an example of notes in time order.)
- Freewrite about your plans for at least five minutes. (See pages 141—142 for an explanation of freewriting and an example.)

b. Find a partner and take turns asking about each other's plans. Add information to your notes as needed.

c. Plan how you will organize the information in your paragraph. You can use time order or listing order. There are models on pages 181 and 183 showing both ways to organize a paragraph about the future.

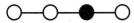

Step 2: Write

Use your notes to write a first draft. Your paragraph must begin with a topic sentence. See the models on page 181 for examples. Your supporting sentences should all relate to your main idea. End your paragraph with a concluding sentence. It should connect to the ideas in your topic sentence. Remember to use *be going to*, not *will*, when you write about your plans for the future.

Step 3: Edit

a. Read your paragraph again. It may help you to read it out loud. Make changes if needed.

b. Edit your paragraph carefully. Check for mistakes before you show it to anyone.

c. Peer review: Exchange papers with a partner. Follow the Reviewer's Checklist on page 198. Check (✓) each box when you finish that step.

d. Return your partner's paper. Say something nice about it.

e. Look at your own paper. If you do not agree with a comment, then ask another student or your teacher.

Reviewer's Checklist — Chapter 9

Your partner's name: _____

<u>Content</u>

☐ Read all of your partner's paragraph.

☐ Underline any part of the paragraph you do not understand. Ask your partner to explain it.

☐ Circle the topic sentence. Write *TS* on the paper if there is no topic sentence.

☐ Reread the supporting sentences. Ask questions if you want more information.

☐ Circle the concluding sentence. Write *CS* on the paper if there is no concluding sentence.

<u>Form</u>

Look at these parts of your partner's paper. Mark any problems on the paper in pencil. Put a question mark (?) if you are not sure about something.

☐ the format of the paper   ☐ the use of verbs with *be going to*

☐ a subject in every sentence   ☐ the use of time-order or

☐ a verb for every subject   listing-order words

 **Step 4: Write the Final Draft**

a. On your first draft, mark any changes you want to make. Then take another piece of paper and write a new draft.

b. Edit your new draft carefully. Then hand it in to your teacher.

Results of the Writing Process

Your teacher may ask you to write another draft after he or she reads your paper. Check your new draft carefully before you hand it in. Remember to hand in your old and new drafts together, with the new draft on top.

When you do not need to rewrite a paragraph anymore, put it in your folder.

Expansion Activities

Your Journal

Continue making entries in your journal. If you cannot think of a topic for a journal entry, try one of these ideas:

- Write about what you are going to do tomorrow. Include at least six activities. Are you looking forward to the day?
- Choose any place in the world and write a weather forecast for this place. Use your imagination, or get current weather information from TV or the Internet.
- Write about the future plans of a friend or family member. Are there going to be any important changes in this person's life? Will this person's plans affect you?
- Write about your life five years from now. Where do you think you will be? What do you think will be different, and what will be the same?
- Write about how you will be learning English in the next few weeks or months. What are you going to continue to do? Are you going to make any changes?

Challenge: *Imagining the Future*

Write a paragraph about future changes. You can write about your country, the environment, fashion, technology, family life, transportation, or another topic of your choosing. Focus on a specific time period — 20 years from now, or 100 years from now, for example — and imagine what life will be like at that time.

Begin with a prewriting activity to gather ideas. Then write a first draft. Begin your paragraph with a topic sentence, and be sure that all your supporting sentences relate to your main idea. Include plenty of details. End your paragraph with a concluding sentence.

Ask a friend or a classmate to review your first draft. Use the Reviewer's Checklist on page 198. Then prepare a final draft and give it to your teacher.

Appendices

Appendix A

The Parts of Speech

The different kinds of words are called **the parts of speech**.

Part of Speech	What is its function?	Examples
a noun	a word for a person, place, thing, or idea	I have a **roommate** at **school**. His **name** is **Mark**. He is from **Hong Kong**. **Mark** and I like the same **music**.
a verb	a word for an action or state	Davina **plays** the guitar and **sings**. She **is** in a band. She **loves** rock music.
an adjective	a word that describes noun or subject pronoun	I have a **new** neighbor named Eva. Eva has a **nice** smile. She is **friendly**.
an adverb	a word that describes a verb, an adjective, another adverb, or a complete sentence, often to tell how, when, or where	The actors talked **fast**. It was **really** difficult to understand them. I listened **very** carefully. I'm going to watch the same movie **tomorrow**. Meet me **here** at 8:00.
a pronoun	a word that takes the place of a noun	Do **you** know Marta? **She** is a good friend of **mine**. **I** like **her** very much.
an article	the word *a, an,* or *the,* used to introduce a noun	There is **a** café on Green Street. **The** café is called *Java's.* It is **an** interesting place.
a preposition	a word that takes a noun or pronoun as an object, often to express a place, time, or direction	I'll meet you **at** 7:30. Let's meet **in front of** the library. We can walk **to** the movie theater.

Appendix B

Subject Pronouns; Object Pronouns; Possessive Adjectives; Possessive Pronouns

Subject Pronouns

Singular	Plural		
I	we	**I** am a student.	**We** are students.
you	you	**You** are my partner.	**You** are my classmates.
he she it	they	**He** is from Japan. **She** is from China. **It** is a chair.	**They** are from Mexico.

Object Pronouns

Singular	Plural		
me	us	Call **me**.	Come with **us**.
you	you	This chair is for **you**.	These chairs are for **you**.
him her it	them	I know **him**. I know **her**. I know **it**.	I know **them**.

Possessive Adjectives

Singular	Plural		
my	our	This is **my** name.	These are **our** names.
your	your	What is **your** name?	What are **your** names?
his her its	their	What is **his** name? What is **her** name? What is **its** name?	What are **their** names?

Possessive Pronouns

Singular	Plural		
mine	ours	This book is **mine**.	This classroom is **ours**.
yours	yours	That book is **yours**.	That classroom is **yours**.
his hers	theirs	That paper is **his**. That paper is **hers**.	That classroom is **theirs**.

Count and Noncount Nouns; Possessive Nouns

Count Nouns

Count nouns can be singular or plural.

Spelling Rules for Plural Count Nouns	Examples
1. For most count nouns, add -*s*.	sister / sister**s** house / house**s**
2. For count nouns ending in *x, ch, sh,* or *ss*, add -*es*.	box / box**es** match / match**es**
3. For most count nouns ending in a consonant + *o*, add -*es*.	tomato / tomato**es** volcano / volcano**es** (Exceptions: photo**s**, piano**s**)
4. For count nouns ending in a vowel + *y*, add -*s*.	boy / boy**s** key / key**s**
5. For count nouns ending in a consonant + *y*, change the *y* to *i* and add -*es*.	baby / bab**ies** party / part**ies**
6. For count nouns ending in *f* or *fe*, drop the *f(e)* and add -*ves*.	knife / kni**ves** wife / wi**ves**

Irregular Count Nouns	Examples	
1. Some count nouns have an irregular plural form.	person / **people** man / **men** tooth / **teeth**	child / **children** woman / **women** foot / **feet**
2. Some count nouns have the same form in the singular and the plural.	fish / **fish**	sheep / **sheep**
3. Some count nouns have only a plural form.	— / **jeans** — / **clothes**	— / **pants** — / **glasses**

Noncount Nouns

Noncount nouns have only one form. These nouns cannot be counted. For example, it is not correct to say *one homework* or *many homeworks*.

Common Noncount Nouns			
Food	**Liquids**	**Substances with Very Small Parts**	**Gases**
bread fruit butter lettuce cheese meat fish soup	coffee oil gasoline soda juice tea milk water	dirt rice dust salt flour sand pepper sugar	air nitrogen helium oxygen hydrogen

Weather	Abstract Ideas	Problems	Other
fog ice rain snow	advice hope education love happiness luck help time	crime noise pollution traffic	e-mail money furniture music homework paper information work

Some nouns (often nouns for food or drink) can be count or noncount:

Count: We would like two **coffees**, please.
Noncount: He drinks a lot of **coffee**.

Possessive Nouns

A **possessive noun** shows the owner of something.

That is **Hiro's** car. = Hiro is the owner of that car. It is his car.

Spelling Rules for Possessive Nouns	Examples
1. Add an apostrophe + *s* (*'s*) to singular nouns.	He is my **sister's** son. I am riding **Carlos's** bike.
2. Add an apostrophe + *s* (*'s*) to plural nouns that do not end in -*s*.	Where is the **men's** department? Tell me the **people's** names.
3. Add an apostrophe alone (') to plural nouns that end in -*s*.	Our **teachers'** offices are on the first floor. The **Smiths'** house is on Maple Street.

Appendix D

The Verb *Be*—Present and Past

The Present of *Be*

Statements: Full Forms

Affirmative Statements		
Subject	***Be***	
I	**am**	ready.
We		
You	**are**	in class.
They		
He		
She	**is**	warm.
It		

Negative Statements			
Subject	***Be***	***Not***	
I	**am**	**not**	late.
We			
You	**are**	**not**	at home.
They			
He			
She	**is**	**not**	cold.
It			

Statements: Contractions

Affirmative
I'm
we're
you're
they're
he's
she's
it's

Negative	
I'm not	—
we're not	we aren't
you're not	you aren't
they're not	they aren't
he's not	he isn't
she's not	she isn't
it's not	it isn't

Questions and Answers

Yes / No Questions		
Be	**Subject**	
Am	I	late?
Are	we	on time?
	you	
	they	
Is	he	ready?
	she	
	it	

Short Answers							
Yes	**Subject**	**Be**		**No**	**Subject**	**Be**	**Not**
Yes,	I	am.		No,	I	am	not.
	we	are.			we	are	
	you				you		
	they				they		
	he	is.			he	is	
	she				she		
	it				it		

Information Questions		
Wh- Question Word	**Be**	
Where	are	we?
Who	is	she?
What	is	that?

Answers
We are on Price Street.
She is my sister.
It is a letter for you.

The Past of *Be*

Statements

Affirmative Statements		
Subject	***Be***	
I	**was**	ready.
We	**were**	in class.
You		
They		
He	**was**	warm.
She		
It		

Negative Statements			
Subject	***Be***	***Not***	
I	**was**	**not**	late.
We	**were**	**not**	at home.
You			
They			
He	**was**	**not**	cold.
She			
It			

Contractions
was + not = **wasn't**
were + not = **weren't**

Questions and Answers

Yes / No Questions		
Be	**Subject**	
Was	I	late?
Were	we	on time?
	you	
	they	
Was	he	ready?
	she	
	it	

Short Answers							
Yes	**Subject**	***Be***		*No*	**Subject**	***Be***	***Not***
Yes,	I	**was.**		No,	I	**was**	not.
	we	**were.**			we	**were**	
	you				you		
	they				they		
	he	**was.**			he	**was**	
	she				she		
	it				it		

Information Questions			Answers
Wh- Question Word	**Be**		
Where	**were**	you?	I was at home.
Who	**was**	that man?	A friend of Rima's.
What	**was**	his name?	Tim.

Appendix E

The Simple Present

Statements

Affirmative Statements		Negative Statements				Contractions
Subject	**Simple Present Verb**	**Subject**	**Do/Does**	**Not**	**Base Form**	
I		I				
We		We				
You	**work.**	You	**do**			do + not = **don't**
They		They		**not**	work.	
He		He				
She	**works.**	She	**does**			does + not = **doesn't**
It		It				

Questions and Answers

Yes / No Questions		
Do / Does	**Subject**	**Base Form**
Do	I	
	we	
	you	
	they	**work**?
Does	he	
	she	
	it	

Short Answers							
Yes	**Subject**	**Do/ Does**		**No**	**Subject**	**Do/ Does**	**Not**
Yes,	I			No,	I		
	we	**do.**			we	**do**	
	you				you		
	they				they		**not.**
	he				he		
	she	**does.**			she	**does**	
	it				it		

Information Questions About the Subject		
Wh- Question Word (subject)	**Simple Present Verb**	
Who	**teaches**	that class?
What	**happens**	on Fridays?

Answers
Ms. Adams.
We go to the lab.

Other Information Questions			
Wh- Question Word	**Do / Does**	**Subject**	**Base Form**
Where	**do**	you	**work**?
Who	**does**	she	**like**?
What	**does**	he	**do**?

Answers
At City Hospital.
Paul.
He is a taxi driver.

Spelling Rules for Third Person Singular Verbs in Affirmative Statements

Rules	Examples
1. For most verbs, add -s to the base form of the verb.	works plays reads writes
2. For verbs ending in *x, ch, sh*, or *ss*, add -*es*.	boxes kisses watches washes
3. For verbs ending in a consonant + *y*, change the *y* to *i* and add -*es*.	study / studies carry / carries fly / flies

Appendix F

The Present Progressive

Statements

Affirmative Statements				Negative Statements			
Subject	***Be***	**Base Form + -*ing***		**Subject**	***Be***	***Not***	**Base Form + -*ing***
I	am			I	am	not	
We				We			
You	are			You	are	not	
They		working.		They			working.
He				He			
She	is			She	is	not	
It				It			

Contractions: *See Appendix D for the contracted forms of* am, is, *and* are.

Questions and Answers

Yes / No Questions		
Be	**Subject**	**Base Form + -ing**
Am	I	
Are	we	
	you	**working**?
	they	
Is	he	
	she	
	it	

Short Answers							
Yes	**Subject**	**Be**		**No**	**Subject**	**Be**	**Not**
	I	**am.**			I	**am**	
	we				we		
	you	**are.**			you	**are**	
Yes,	they			No,	they		**not.**
	he				he		
	she	**is.**			she	**is**	
	it				it		

Information Questions About the Subject				Answers
Wh- Question Word (subject)	**Is**	**Base Form + -ing**		
Who	**is**	**singing**?		Janice is.
What	**is**	**happening**?		We are having a meeting.

Other Information Questions					Answers
Wh- Question Word	**Be**	**Subject**	**Base Form + -ing**		
Where	**are**	you	**going**?		To work.
Who	**is**	she	**calling**?		Her mother.
What	**is**	he	**doing**?		He is fixing the computer.

Spelling Rules for Verbs Ending in *-ing*

Rules	Examples
1. Add *-ing* to the base form of most verbs.	go / go**ing** read / read**ing** fly / fly**ing**
2. When the base form ends in *e*, drop the *e* and add *-ing*.	mak**e** / mak**ing** writ**e** / writ**ing**
3. When the base form ends in *ie*, change the *ie* to *y* and add *-ing*.	d**ie** / d**ying** l**ie** / l**ying**
4. When the last three letters of the base form are consonant + vowel + consonant, double the final consonant and add *-ing*.	be**gin** / begi**nning** sto**p** / sto**pping**
5. There are two exceptions to Rule 4: • Do not double *w* or *x*. • Do not double the final consonant when the last syllable is not stressed.	snowing fixing listening offering happening

Appendix G — The Simple Past

Regular Verbs in the Simple Past

Affirmative Statements		Negative Statements				Contractions
Subject	**Simple Past Verb**	**Subject**	***Did***	***Not***	**Base Form**	
I		I				
We		We				
You		You				
They	**worked.**	They	**did**	**not**	work.	
He		He				did + not = **didn't**
She		She				
It		It				

Questions and Answers

Yes / No Questions		
Did	Subject	Base Form
Did	I we you they he she it	**work**?

Short Answers							
Yes	Subject	*Did*		*No*	Subject	*Did*	*Not*
Yes,	I we you they he she it	**did**.		No,	I we you they he she it	**did**	**not**.

Information Questions About the Subject		
Wh- Question Word (subject)	Simple Past Verb	
Who	**worked**	yesterday?
What	**happened**	on Friday?

Answers
I did.
We watched a movie in class.

Other Information Questions			
Wh- Question Word	*Did*	Subject	Base Form
Where	**did**	you	**walk**?
Who	**did**	she	**call**?
What	**did**	he	**do**?

Answers
In the park.
Her sister.
He washed his car.

Spelling Rules for Verbs Ending in *-ed*

Rules	Examples
1. Add *-ed* to the base form of most regular verbs.	watch**ed** play**ed** listen**ed**
2. When the base form ends in *e*, then add *-d* only.	danc**ed** hop**ed** believ**ed**
3. When the base form ends in a consonant + *y*, drop the *y* and add *-ied*.	stu**dy** / stud**ied** car**ry** / carr**ied**
4. When the base form ends in consonant + vowel + consonant, then double the final consonant and add *-ed*.	p**lan** / plan**ned** s**hop** / shop**ped** pre**fer** / prefer**red**
5. There are two exceptions to Rule 4: • Do not double *w* or *x*. • Do not double the final consonant when the last syllable is not stressed.	snowed mixed relaxed *Stressed*: re**fer** / refer**red** *Not stressed*: offer / offer**ed**

Irregular Verbs in the Simple Past

For *be*:   See Appendix D.

Affirmative statements: See the Irregular Verbs chart in Appendix H.

Negative statements: Irregular verbs are the same as regular verbs in negative statements.

Questions: For information questions about the subject, use the irregular verb forms shown in Appendix H. Irregular verbs are the same as regular verbs in *yes/no* questions and other information questions.

Appendix H

Irregular Verbs

Base Form	Simple Past	Base Form	Simple Past
be	was / were	keep	kept
become	became	know	knew
begin	began	leave	left
blow	blew	let	let
break	broke	lose	lost
bring	brought	make	made
build	built	pay	paid
buy	bought	put	put
catch	caught	quit	quit
choose	chose	ride	rode
come	came	ring	rang
cost	cost	run	ran
cut	cut	say	said
do	did	see	saw
draw	drew	sell	sold
drink	drank	set	set
drive	drove	shake	shook
eat	ate	shoot	shot
fall	fell	shut	shut
feel	felt	sing	sang
fight	fought	sit	sat
find	found	sleep	slept
fit	fit	speak	spoke
fly	flew	spend	spent
forget	forgot	stand	stood
get	got	steal	stole
give	gave	swim	swam
go	went	take	took
grow	grew	teach	taught
have	had	tell	told
hear	heard	think	thought
hide	hid	throw	threw
hit	hit	understand	understood
hurt	hurt	write	wrote

Appendix 1   Expressing Future Time with *Be Going To* and *Will*

Be Going To

Statements

Affirmative Statements				Negative Statements	Contractions
Subject	**Be**	***Going To***	**Base Form**		
I	**am**			Add *not* after *am*, *is*, or *are*.	See Appendix D for the contracted forms of *am*, *is*, and *are*.
We	**are**				
You					
They		**going to**	**eat.**		
He					
She	**is**				
It					

Questions and Answers

Yes / No Questions				Short Answers
Be	**Subject**	***Going To***	**Base Form**	
Am	I			
	we			
Are	you			See Appendix D for the short answers for questions with *be* in the present tense.
	they	**going to**	**eat?**	
	he			
Is	she			
	it			

Information Questions About the Subject				Answers
Wh- Question Word (subject)	*Is*	*Going To*	Base Form	
Who	**is**	**going to**	**help?**	John is.
What	**is**	**going to**	**happen?**	We are going to take a vote.

Other Information Questions					Answers
Wh- Question Word	*Be*	Subject	*Going To*	Base Form	
Where	**are**	you	**going to**	**go?**	To the beach.
Who	**is**	she	**going to**	**invite?**	All the neighbors.
What	**is**	he	**going to**	**do?**	He is going to find a new job.

Will

Statements

Affirmative Statements			Negative Statements				Contractions	
Subject	*Will*	Base Form	Subject	*Will*	*Not*	Base Form	Affirmative	Negative
I			I				**I'll**	
We			We				**we'll**	
You			You				**you'll**	
They	**will**	**work.**	They	**will**	**not**	work.	**they'll**	will + not = **won't**
He			He				**he'll**	
She			She				**she'll**	
It			It				**it'll**	

Questions and Answers

Yes / No Questions				Short Answers							
Will	**Subject**	**Base Form**		**Yes**	**Subject**	*Will*		**No**	**Subject**	*Will*	*Not*
Will	I	work?		Yes,	I	will.		No,	I	will	not.
	we				we				we		
	you				you				you		
	they				they				they		
	he				he				he		
	she				she				she		
	it				it				it		

Information Questions About the Subject				Answers
Wh- Question Word (subject)	*Will*	**Base Form**		
Who	**will**	**help**	tomorrow?	Mary will.
What	**will**	**happen**	next Monday?	There will be a meeting.

Other Information Questions				Answers
Wh- Question Word	*Will*	**Subject**	**Base Form**	
Where	**will**	the concert	**be?**	In the park.
Who	**will**	he	**call?**	His doctor.
What	**will**	they	**do?**	They will sell the car.

Appendix J — Order of Adjectives

There can be more than one adjective before a noun, as in

There is a <u>nice</u> <u>new</u> <u>Vietnamese</u> restaurant on Main Street.

Adjectives usually go in this order before a noun:

Categories of adjectives	Size	Opinion	Physical Description			Origin	Material
			Shape	Age	Color		
Examples of adjectives	big small	good beautiful expensive	round square	old new	red white light blue	English African Japanese	plastic cotton wooden

They live in a beautiful old apartment building.

He drives a small white Korean car.

Use commas + *and* or *or* when you use a series of three adjectives from the same category.

The orange, white, and green flag of Ivory Coast is similar to the Irish flag.

There are no French, German, or Spanish students in the class.

Never put a comma between the last adjective in a series and the noun.

Appendix K — Sentence Types

There are three basic types of sentences: simple, compound, and complex.

Simple Sentences

A simple sentence has one subject-verb combination. See page 103 for examples of simple sentences.

Compound Sentences

A compound sentence has two subject-verb combinations (simple sentence + simple sentence). See page 143 for examples of compound sentences.

A compound sentence needs a comma and a coordinating conjunction to connect the simple sentences. There are seven coordinating conjunctions:

Coordinating Conjunctions

and	but	for	nor	or	so	yet

Complex Sentences

A complex sentence has one independent clause and one or more dependent clauses.

- An independent clause can stand alone. It can be a simple sentence.

  Examples: We didn't go.

                I will call you.

                He watches the news.

- A dependent clause cannot stand alone because it does not express a complete thought.

  Examples: because it was raining

                when I get home

                if he has time

Examples of Complex Sentences

Independent clause + dependent clause	Dependent clause, independent clause
We didn't go because it was raining.	Because it was raining, we didn't go.
I will call you when I get home.	When I get home, I will call you.
He watches the news if he has time.	If he has time, he watches the news.

A dependent clause has a subordinating conjunction + subject + verb. There are many subordinating conjunctions.

Examples of Subordinating Conjunctions

For Adverb Clauses			For Adjective Clauses			
Time	**Reason**	**Condition**	**People**	**Things**	**Times**	**Places**
as soon as after before when	because since	if unless	who whom that	that which	when	where

Appendix L — Rules for Capitalization

When to Use a Capital Letter

1. At the beginning of a sentence

2. For the pronoun *I*

3. For people's names and titles (Do not capitalize a title without a name: *Where does the queen live?*)

4. For: nationalities
   languages
   religions
   ethnic groups

5. For place names (such as specific countries, cities, rivers, mountains, and so on)

6. For names of buildings, roads, bridges, and other structures

7. For names of months, holidays, special time periods, and the days of the week
   (Do not capitalize the seasons: *winter, spring, summer, fall/autumn.*)

Examples

My name is Merita. **W**hat is your name?

Hassan and **I** are partners.

My dentist's name is **D**r. **P**arker.
This is a picture of **Q**ueen **E**lizabeth.

Canadian, **S**yrian, **B**razilian
English, **A**rabic, **P**ortuguese
Buddhism, **I**slam, **C**hristianity
Native **A**merican, **L**atino

Miami, **F**lorida, is in the **U**nited **S**tates.
Where are the **R**ocky **M**ountains?

That building is the **W**estin **H**otel.
My bank is on **H**igh **S**treet.
We saw the **S**tatue of **L**iberty.

There are thirty days in **A**pril.
Do you celebrate **N**ew **Y**ear's **E**ve?
When is **R**amadan?
My appointment is on **M**onday.

8. For names of organizations (such as businesses, schools, clubs)

My country belongs to the **U**nited **N**ations.
He is the president of **N**ike.
She is a student at **H**arvard.

9. For abbreviations

He drives a red **VW**.
They are students at **UCLA**.

10. For the titles of movies, TV shows, plays, books, newspapers, and magazines

• Capitalize the first word and all nouns, pronouns, verbs, adjectives, and adverbs.

Have you seen *Gone with the Wind*?
Who wrote *A Raisin in the Sun*?

• Use *italics* when you write a title on the computer.

I used to watch *Sesame Street*.

• <u>Underline</u> a title when you write it by hand.

He reads <u>The Boston Globe</u> every day.

11. For the titles of your paragraphs
See page 90.

My **H**ometown
Planning for the **F**uture

Appendix M   Punctuation

Punctuation Mark	Rules for Use	Examples
period	1. Use at the end of a statement.	My name is Anna.
	2. Use to separate dollars and cents.	$10.99
question mark	Use at the end of a question.	What is your name?
exclamation point	1. Use to show surprise or strong emotion.	What a nice idea!
	2. Use to show a command is strong.	Don't forget!
apostrophe	1. Use in place of a letter in a contraction.	he + is = he's
	2. Use to form a possessive noun.	That is Mr. King's office.
quotation marks	Use before and after the exact words that someone spoke.	He said, "Meet me at 4:00."

Punctuation Mark	Rules for Use	Examples
comma	1. Use between the date and the year and also after the year in a sentence.	It happened on July 4, 1776. May 1, 2001, was my first day on the job.
	2. Use after an introductory word or phrase at the beginning of a sentence.	Finally, add salt and pepper. On Friday, they met for lunch.
	3. Use to separate three or more items in a series.	I like bananas, apples, oranges, and pears.
	4. Use after the first part of a compound sentence.	He loves good food, but he does not like to cook.
	5. Use after a dependent clause that comes first in a complex sentence.	After the class ended, we went for coffee.
	6. Use in large numbers to separate thousands, millions, billions, and so on.	There are 5,280 feet in a mile. She received $2,000,000.

Appendix N

Correction Symbols

Group 1

Symbol	Meaning	Example of Error
cap.	capitalization error	The class meets on <u>m</u>onday. *(cap.)*
pl.	plural	She has two <u>book</u>. *(pl.)*
sp.	spelling mistake	He is a <u>colege</u> student. *(sp.)*
∧	missing word	He ∧ my friend.
——	rewrite as shown	I go with ~~my some~~ friends. *(some of my)*

I would like to introduce myself. <u>my</u> name is Isabel Angara. *(cap.)*

I ∧ from the Philippines. I ∧ married. I have one son and one <u>daugther</u>. *(sp.)* *(am taking)*

I ~~take~~ two classes. I want to learn <u>e</u>nglish. I want to study <u>computer</u>. *(cap.)* *(pl.)*

Group 2

Symbol	Meaning	Example of Error
w.w.	wrong word	He makes cars in a Honda <u>fabric</u>. (w.w.)
~	wrong word order	It is a restaurant nice.
⊘	delete word	Do you like the hip-hop music?
agr.	error in subject-verb agreement	You <u>was</u> absent yesterday. (agr.)
‿	connect or close up space	I some times watch the news. He speaks English, Spanish , and French .

Alessandro Santos has a life very busy. He <u>has</u> (w.w.) nineteen years old.

He is a college student, and he works, too. He delivers the pizzas

for Pizza Express. He <u>have</u> (agr.) classes during the week, and he <u>work</u> (agr.) on

week ends. He <u>is</u> (w.w.) not have much time free. Sometimes he is plays

basket ball with his friends.

Group 3

Symbol	Meaning	Example of Error
p.	punctuation error	She was born on March, 13, 1987. (p.)
v.t.	wrong verb tense	Last night, I <u>see</u> a good movie. (v.t.)
w.f.	wrong word form	We are going <u>shop</u> downtown. (w.f.)
FRAG	sentence fragment	I went home. Because I was tired. (FRAG)
RO	run-on sentence	He gets up early he takes a shower. (RO)

I <u>have</u> (v.t.) a scary experience two years ago I was in a car accident. (RO) The

other driver did not stop at a stop sign, so his car <u>hitting</u> (w.f.) my car.

When he ran into me. (FRAG) My car turned, and hit another car. (p.) I was very

<u>scary</u> (w.f.). There was a lot of damage to the cars but no one was <u>bad</u> (w.f.) hurt. (p.)

Index